HOW TO
SPOOK
YOURSELF
K
P
U

A MANUAL FOR
PARANORMAL
INVESTIGATION

TERESA L CAROL

Denise!
Celebrate your
fabulous Psychic
gift. Love that man of
yours!
Teresa Carol
8/24/19

Published by
Doce Blant Publishing, Federal Way, WA 98387
www.doceblantpublishing.com

Cover by Fiona Jayde Media
Interior Design by The Deliberate Page

Paperback ISBN: 978-1-7320807-6-8
Hardbound ISBN: 978-0-9994937-2-4
Ebook ISBN: 978-1-7320807-7-5

Library of Congress Control Number 2018950232

Printed in the United States of America
www.doceblant.com

CONTENTS

I. INTRODUCTION

So, you want to be a Ghost Buster? While it's exciting to think of exploring an old haunted mansion or traipsing through a graveyard, let's look at this from a more professional level. It's important to realize the impact that you can have on someone's life. Can you imagine how you might feel if someone intruded into your sanctuary and declared that they had discovered a demon? Then, after dropping that emotionally charged bomb, they just left as if it should be no problem at all.

Basically, what we see on many of these ghost hunting television shows is a group of reactive investigators who jump at every noise, scream at the apparent ghost, make random determinations, tag the property haunted, and then go off to their next grand adventure.

As you can imagine—depending on the owner's superstitions and beliefs—there could be all forms of consequences. I have heard of people paying supposed demonologists as much as $10,000 to cleanse a property. Many people sell the house at a financial loss just to get out of it. Children are uprooted and farmed off to live with relatives. Terrified mates often have little or no sympathy from their skeptical partners who may even ridicule their fears. Can you imagine how overwhelming it would be if your sanctuary became a place of constant dread?

What about the ghost? There doesn't seem to be any Association for the Protection and Respect of Paranormal Beings. So, what about their rights? They are people too, even though they may be technically dead. Shouldn't they be treated with some measure of respect? If they are haunting a location, don't you think they are dealing with their own sense of trauma? Why would you make their world more uncomfortable by reacting disrespectfully to them?

Oh, yes, there is nothing more embarrassing than to get caught up in the hysteria of the moment and later to find that the so-called demon was a bat in the attic, or a tree rubbing the gutters. Heh, heh, heh. It's always best to rule out the obvious.

Visiting a potentially haunted property needs a level head, a game plan, and a determination to discover the truth of what's really going on. Hysteria and sensationalism have no part in a professional investigation.

Document, document, document! In my early years, I knew of no one doing paranormal investigations, and to me it was often just a hoot and a holler. "Really? Let's check it out!" Now I wish I had written down details, taken photographs and listed contacts. But I learned from experience that investigations without factual information are just good stories.

I listen to people talking about their interests in the hidden or metaphysical realities and, half the time, they are hearing each other, but not understanding each other. Okay! That's probably true of most conversations; however, I notice this tendency is more extreme in my field, as metaphysical subjects are not uniformly taught. For that matter, metaphysics is not widely taught. This is big, and much of what is ascribed to metaphysics is often sensationalized with a gooey coating of superstition and fear. Easy to do when few truly know what's what in the spiritual realms.

Terminology for any subject is like a slang of its own. Personally, I prefer not to put so much effort into explaining myself, only to find that the listener has a skewed idea about what I'm describing. Therefore, I normally begin most of my dialogues with clarification of metaphysical terms. For this reason, you will find an index of terms at the back of this manual.

Metaphysics is the study of that which is to be found beyond the physical. It is the modern term for the unseen realities that have not yet been scientifically explained. It is a broad term and takes in almost everything, including ghosts, auric fields, vortexes, dimensions, and spiritual phenomena.

Spirituality is an active, intimate relationship with God. On the other hand, religion is a path that another individual has successfully used to achieve this connection with God. Spirituality is living the relationship; religion is seeking the relationship. Not all spiritual people are religious nor are all religious individuals spiritual. I consider myself spiritual and, although I came to this level of intimacy with God through religion, I no longer think of myself as a religious person.

Because there is so much that is unknown about the spiritual realms, a writer such as Dante with his fantasy classic, The Divine Comedy, specifically, The Inferno: The Immortal Drama of a Journey through Hell, can influence the thinking of the community at large. It is interesting to speak to religious people and to hear how many of their religious ideas are from creative writings and paintings that have nothing to do with sacred scriptures. Those who are familiar with the Bible know that Hell or Sheol is a fiery furnace used for burning the impure elements out of the soul. It is not, as many believe, a fiery pit of eternal suffering populated with devils and demons. Putting a demon near fire is much the same as putting a cat in water. If you survive the experience, you will definitely know that demons don't like fire any more than cats like water. But such ideas of Hell serve to manipulate the uneducated through fear and misunderstandings.

Superstition and fear are the greatest handicaps to understanding the spiritual realms. Those who have the ability to perceive the spiritual worlds are often persecuted by individuals that have no awareness of what lies behind the veil. Beliefs about the spiritual realms and psychic seers can be highly erroneous or judgmental. Being psychic is either deemed the Gift of God or the Curse of the Devil. In truth, it may be the combo deal, but it's a part of our human nature and I would encourage you to develop it.

II. Professionalism

Every business has certain "dos and don'ts," which comprise professional ethics. Most of these values are standard in every industry, and, so, I would ask you to stop and realize, as a Paranormal Investigator, you are representing a service industry and need to establish a personal level of integrity. In other words: define what's okay and what's not.

1. **Zero drugs or alcohol** - first and foremost—no exceptions—this means all team members, and this also includes the property owner and their guests. Drugs and alcohol lure in disagreeable spirits and the last thing you need is a drunk shouting profanity and trying to push someone down the stairs. Besides, people who are using have the tendency to be noisy and intrusive, and it is impossible to get clean recordings with someone staggering around the house slamming doors and yelling, "Here ghostie, ghostie!"

I did an investigation in Olympia some years back where all the women huddled, teary eyed and fearful, in the kitchen, drinking wine coolers, while the men stomped and cussed on the front porch, passing the bong around. I discovered their eight-year-old child upstairs in her closet so frightened that she had wet herself. "Hello adults!" And the ghosties, they decided to clear out for the night, it was just too much for them.

2. **Privacy policy** - come on! Anywhere you go, now, someone slips a confidentiality form under your nose to read and initial. It's a time of not disclosing other people's private business. You can share your stories and reports generically, but no personal information, no address, and no names: nothing that would identify the client. They are already feeling vulnerable. Let's be respectful and maintain the trust they have in our ability to assist them. Let's keep their personal business confidential.

3. **Don't open drawers or closets** - if you need to see something personal, ask the client to come in and show it to you. Let them handle the item and insist that they secure it before you leave the room. I once finished an investigation, and the husband came out to my car with a printout of all the personal effects that I had supposedly stolen. I got out of the car and called the police. I filed the police report because they were refusing payment claiming I stole from them. I didn't get paid on this job, but at least I stopped a more serious problem from developing.

4. **Don't set yourself up to be someone else's scapegoat** - In the early 1990's I went to a rental home that the occupants claimed had the spirit of a voodoo priest tormenting their children. They refused to accompany me into the house, even though the children were supposedly sleeping inside. As I was standing at the front door, my assistant noticed that the father had just thrown a

bag into the back of the pickup truck we had driven to the location. We left immediately and found, bloody undergarments for a child inside the bag. We called the police and they gathered the evidence. The children were removed from the home the next day and later adopted by foster parents. I was summoned to testify at two separate hearings. Had I hesitated, we could have left fingerprints and been falsely accused of a crime.

5. **Don't antagonize the pets** - One of the major reasons to do an Initial Interview is to determine if there are any animals or children in the house. Easy going dogs can attack if they feel someone is upsetting their family, and one seemingly innocent reaction can lead to a hysterical episode where someone gets bit. Birds are territorial and curious. I once had a macaw land on my shoulder and rip an earring out. Oh, yes, and the snake room—I almost had a major accident! Best rule of thumb: All pets are fully secured before the investigators enter the premise. Know what you are walking into.

6. **Beware of the effect that the investigation has on the children** - I have had countless adults tell me of how horrifying their childhood was because they had to sleep in a room where someone saw a ghost. Parents may minimize their child's concerns, but you are the adult and you need to be conscientious. Don't say anything that might traumatize anyone. There is no way to fully understand the long term emotional impact on a child, or fear of the unknown. If children are present, I often point out to them that it is normal for old houses to have squeaky spots, and that faucets drip and trees

can scratch the sides of the house, making a spooky sound. But I also try to give them skills such as, "Take a deep breath. Now, have your guides and angels walk with you." If I feel that a child is upset, I make sure the parent realizes this and offer solutions, such as watching TV programs like Casper the Friendly Ghost or the Ghost and Mrs. Muir. Talking about angels and grandparents, who are on the other side, can be exceptionally helpful. It's great if you have a psychologist on the team, or at least one you can consult with. Never leave someone in trauma. Even more important, don't drive them there in the first place.

7. **Don't scare off the ghost or phenomena** - There are conscious beings such as earth divas, ghosts, entity attachments, and so on. If they know you're looking to take them out, you can pretty much count on the fact that they will disappear until you are gone. It's no fun to spend hours combing through a house to find nothing, and then, afterward, get a call telling you that when your team left, the problem returned with renewed ferocity. If you discuss the phenomena at the Initial Interview, you, in most cases, won't be overheard. I tell the client not to talk about the phenomena until we have done a "cold" walk through. This does a lot to defuse hysteria and, besides, the less talking, the easier it is to get good recordings.

8. **Be considerate of the living** - This is someone's home—you don't need to clutter it with gory images of someone hanging in the stairwell, mutilated on the kitchen table or suffocated in their bed. Just like the pink elephant, how do you un-see it once someone has

told you that it's there? There is more than one way to say something. Say it professionally with as little trauma as you can.

9. **Be respectful to the dead** - No yelling at the dead, "you're dead!" That's just cold. How would you feel if I said that to you? You'd either think I was crazy and needed to be avoided or that it was a threat, like saying, "you're so dead, I'm going to kill you." Either way it's upsetting for the ghosts. Imagine how an Earth Spirit might feel: "Wow, this person thinks I'm dead, let's follow her home and torment her." Oh, yeah, the gutter that came loose doesn't really care, it never was truly alive—just a little unhinged.

10. **Take pride in your work** - This is an amazing chance you have to take a look at the spiritual realms. Why not take the time, do the documentation, and figure things out? It's so satisfying when you have learned from experience, can clear out a house, and bring comfort to someone that has been spooked-up. Take your time and keep focused on what you are up to, and how you are handling it.

11. **No Bragging** - I was once part of a large group of paranormal investigators that spent a weekend together. The first night there was some serious partying going on and everyone was sending out electronic posts. Well, it led to a major misrepresentation of the group as a whole. I can't speak for everyone, but I know most teams, including mine were in professional mode during the actual investigation, but much of the Facebook and Messenger posts made it appear that we were all

running around in a drunken stupor. Not the image I wanted put out there. Wait until the event is over to post, and be clear about events and provide clear timelines when posting to the general public.

Here are three important questions you need to ask yourself and your team before you go out on any investigation:

1. **Why am I here?** Has the property owner invited you to see what you can see? Are you and a group of buddies just checking out a property that has been reported as haunted? So, do you intend to do a documentable investigation or just run around and react to any unexplained phenomena without a set plan? And what about follow-up and resolution of the situation? Do you intend to be respectful and supportive of the property owner, as well as the ghosties?

2. **Do I have any idea of what to look for?** Have you taken time to do an Initial Interview and gathered relevant information about the occurrences? Have you met with the property owner and assessed if there are any dangers? Could there be a hoax? A mental health issue? What types of phenomena are being experienced? Could there be a vortex? A ghost? A nature spirit? Or (suck in your breath and make the shocked face) a demon!

3. **Are you prepared?** Are you going in with an educated, levelheaded, respectful group of experienced Paranormal Investigators, who will be able to support you in making an assessment and assist you with cures?

Do you have a plan that will minimize the hysteria and miscommunications, and defuse any uncomfortable situations? Can you honestly handle this? If not, who is your back up?

Make It Professional

Okay, if you plan to do this professionally, then take the time and attend to the following as it will save you a lot of problems later:

- Decide what exact service you offer.
  - » Investigation
  - » House Blessing and Balancing of Energies throughout the property
  - » Ghost and Paranormal Clearing
  - » In depth documentation compiled in a report
  - » All of the above

- State Business License—don't fret about taxes—you have to make a lot of money before you start paying, but a business license adds to your professionalism and keeps things legal. It's good to know the law.

- Decide how much you plan to charge or whether you'll accept donations.

- Have a clear policy on how the money is divided.
  - » Quarterly dinner meetings
  - » Gas, hotel, travel expenses
  - » Booth fees at local Paranormal Trade Shows
  - » New Team Equipment such as team uniforms, cameras etc.

- » Stationary and business cards.
- » Batteries

- Name your business; make a logo and a mission statement and business forms.

- Establish a Dress Code for your team.

- Provide nametags for your team.

- Build a clean reputation

- Know your team. Are they all on the same page and with the same level of integrity? Team members with different ideas can tear a team apart or worse, cause a lawsuit.
  - » Take pride in your work.
  - » Advertise your service clearly and follow through

- Share your knowledge. Educate your clients and the public in general, but most importantly, educate your team.

- Seek experience and education. I require that anyone who accompanies me to an investigation has at least sat through one class with me. I have enough to tend to without having to train someone as I go, or worse yet, defuse any misinformation that might terrify the client.

III. Protection

Protection is a major concern for people awakening to their spiritual path. When individuals come to me for psychic readings or spiritual education, they are often inhibited by concerns of what terrible things they might encounter in the unknown. People tell me about their spiritual abilities and how they have shut themselves down because they are afraid of evil. I have found that more harm comes to individuals through their own superstition and fear than they would ever encounter in the spiritual realms.

I often talk about being safe, which, I have later realized, may create a sense of unease for anyone unfamiliar with the spiritual realms. A modern mind may wander to one of many fabulously animated movies, complete with horrors beyond imagination. If such science fiction were really true, I, for one, would remain safely closeted behind locked doors. Just remember, where movies are concerned, we know that dancing lollypops aren't real, but when we don't know, as in the case of most spiritual phenomena, we have the tendency to react out of fear. When I speak of safety, it is in the same vein as safe sex, safe driving and conscientious child supervision. To be safe is to use common sense and be aware of the surroundings.

Education and experience are two of the best protections a modern-day paranormal investigator can have. But getting either is challenging. Paranormal investigation—an ancient art—is grossly steeped in superstition and false fears. In addition, in the past, very little accurate information has been made available to the general public.

Now, I'm not saying that caution is not required. An individual exploring the spiritual realms can be similar to a child experimenting with a pair of tweezers. It is not that the electrical outlet is harmful. If used appropriately, it is totally safe. Yet, to the unaware child, the tweezers look like a custom fit for the outlet, and, without supervision, of course, a child will most likely plug them in. So it is with someone immature in his exploration of the spiritual realm—he will often severely shock himself, and then deem the spiritual realm as dangerous.

The most important thing to realize is that we are all spiritually safe. In this, I mean that we are eternal, and therefore, as Eternal Beings, anything we experience is only temporary. Scientists have proved that energy cannot die; it merely transforms itself into another form. The human soul is the same—it cannot die; it just moves on. Different religions give an explanation for this process as: reincarnation, life in another world, or resurrection. Whether we understand it or not, we are eternal and cannot be fatally harmed.

We also have spiritual allies: angels, spirit guides, ancestors, and master teachers, which we will encounter once we begin to explore the unseen worlds. There are endless accounts of these otherworldly beings and their willingness to assist us.

The term, "spiritual realms" seems to be a catchall phrase for anywhere nonphysical. I prefer the term metaphysical, which means beyond the physical. The spiritual realms and this physical reality are interconnected in the same way that the cardiovascular and the nervous system citizens from revolting under the dictatorship of those who claimed they were chosen by God.

My experience with demons and devils has been limited, but my understanding is that they are living beings of the Angelic Realms. They are quite large, approximately six feet tall. They have the appearance of being half ape and half shaggy dog. Their coats are dark in color, and their hands and feet are dark-skinned and human-like in appearance. Although their tails are dog-like in form, they are prehensile, which allows them to grip with them, similar to monkeys. Demons have dark black animal eyes and the fanged teeth of predators. They live in another reality, and are highly family oriented and extremely territorial. They are aggressive when trapped, but by nature they tend to flee unless protecting their kill or their young.

It would be rare for any human to encounter a demon while in the physical realm, as they are not commonly found in this reality. Yet, there are enough stories to indicate that there may have been a time when demons were present on the earth. Demons, of their own accord, are not curious and do not wander far from their lairs. Therefore, I am extremely cautious when I see one in the spiritual realm, as it was most likely trapped and brought to that location. My greatest apprehension is about the person who would want to trap and release a demon. It reminds me of the 1994 movie, *Color of Night*, where actor, Bruce Willis, opens the mail box to find a rattlesnake inside. What kind of individual would put a rattlesnake in someone's mailbox? And what will they do next? As for the demon, it's like the rattlesnake—it has no intention of harming anyone—it just wants to be left alone, but it will defend itself if trapped.

As to the vulnerability of the average person, I have to be honest, unless a person has some position of power or is creating pain for others, most of us don't give him a second thought. As long as an individual doesn't provoke another or place himself in an obviously dangerous situation, he's safe. I can't imagine anyone intentionally seeking out and provoking a demon or a rattle snake. Just as in the real world, the spiritual world operates on the same principals. The spiritual realm is safe; it's just unknown and, therefore, can appear intimidating.

Because of our imagination, when we don't know what we're dealing with, we find a scary situation more frightening. We fear what's out there, not knowing if we can survive the unknown. As soon as it becomes clear that we're facing only a crocodile or an alien, we immediately begin to strategize. We now know our safety zone and how to protect ourselves. In the same way, understanding the spiritual realms and what's out there gives us the awareness that we are safe, and how to keep ourselves from harm.

So, how can you know the truth when it comes to Satan, demons, devils, and evil? How can you know what is true?

Your own higher self knows, and the Divine Spirit will guide you, if you seek the truth. It is important to keep an open heart, an open mind, and a yearning for God. With these three elements, that which is truth will ring so strongly within you that there will be no doubt. Fear will keep you from the truth, so be clear that your knowing comes from experience, not as a reaction to the superstition of others.

To be safe in the spiritual realms, the most important things to remember are: common sense, good guidance, and communion with the Divine Spirit. The best way to develop these three is to have a healthy spiritual coach, make sacred time to experience and to do the diligence of meditation, and listen as you ask for spiritual guidance.

rushing through the house, slamming doors and flicking lights, while the lady of the house screams in horror, her children sob, clinging to her skirt, and her husband charges at me, yelling at the top of his lungs that I have upset his family.

Honestly, I prefer not to let things get *that* out of hand. So, I come prepared. I also take time to prepare my clients. Therefore, I seldom have to deal with such melodramatics. If there should be any rushing, slamming, flickering, screaming, sobbing, charging or yelling—it will be me. I'm a bit of a scaredy-cat, especially with physical trauma. Spiritual stuff doesn't spook me…much.

When my associates and I arrive at a property, we park in a highly visible location, which I call the get-away position. This is a location where there are neighbors and traffic. If it becomes necessary, this makes it easy to send someone to the car on the pretext of getting a gismo, and frees them to call for the police or holler for assistance. This is so that if something becomes awkward (like when a gun toting boyfriend physically threatened us, as in *The Case of the Hidden Tunnel)*, we can get away immediately. Whenever I am concerned there might be physical danger, we often arrive in separate vehicles or have a driver waiting in the car. I will also bring someone along that I humorously call, the "bouncer," who is trained to handle people in physically reactive situations.

Regardless, of whether I perceive danger or not, my associates and I always have a set of subtle emergency signals. The one signal I have used most often is pulling my nose. This is the signal for "*Run!*" Rarely, but it has been known to happen, the ghost is there as a permanent guest of someone currently living in the house. Like, in *The Case of the Ghost Children*, the client is unaware that someone they are living with has buried a body on the premise. My policy is to make sure that all residents know when I am coming. This minimizes the chance of any surprises, and I am great at taking "hints" of where not to look. In other words, if someone tells you to "stay out" of a given location, stay out!

THE DANGERS OF PARANORMAL INVESTIGATION

Paranormal investigation is dangerous primarily because of the living. Sometimes there is an individual who has a secret that he wants left undisturbed. Or, most commonly, there are people who become triggered by the highly charged emotional environment of the investigation. Often their fight or flight response switches to fight. More than once, I have had an enraged husband come charging after me, certain I created their problem. Because of this I never make my home address available to my clients and I come prepared to flee if things begin to feel perilous.

In 1988, after several conversations with the police over someone who was harassing me, I was advised to take handgun lessons and carry one. I had come home to find all my doors wide open and a note scrawled in lipstick on the bathroom mirror, "Back off Bitch!" After that, at two separate restaurants, where I was featured doing psychic readings, I entered the ladies' restroom to find the identical message scrawled in my lipstick on the bathroom mirror.

Later that month, an old pickup truck followed me from Tacoma to Vancouver, Washington. That night, someone left a message at the hotel desk where I was staying that advised me "Don't go back, Bitch!"

The stalking started shortly after I had visited a property where a distraught mother kept seeing children playing on her lawn. What was even more remarkable was when photos were taken with the house as a backdrop, the faces of children could be seen looking out of the windows.

The client, who called me, had recently remarried, and her 17-year-old teenager had run off, after the girl had a hostile fight with her new stepfather. Within the following week, the girl's mother was having strange dreams, hearing sounds in the house, and seeing the ghost children playing on the lawn. It was apparent that the mother's distress over her daughter leaving put her in a highly emotional state, and thus made it possible for her to view the ghost children, who had apparently died in the local area over one hundred years ago.

When I met with the woman and her sister at a local coffee shop, I felt no reason for concern but decided to include a psychologist in my premise investigation team. I felt the woman had avoided dealing with her daughter's abrupt departure. She appeared almost hysterical, yet she insisted her daughter had run off with her boyfriend. This took place nine months after the incident, and her daughter was 18 years old, but she still had heard nothing from her.

When we arrived at the house, the husband was not present. I felt a strong foreboding. I felt it again as I began to investigate the daughter's old room, which had been turned into a study for the husband. The same apprehensive feeling resurfaced when I came across the vegetable garden he had started in the back yard.

After clearing the house and property of ghosts, and giving the woman pamphlets on seeking assistance in time of loss and abandonment, I proceeded to give her a summation of my findings. I had discovered, although not on her property, but within a city block of the location, that a structure had collapsed in the 1890's. This fatal accident killed five sleeping children, all of which had been buried in her back yard, most likely where the new garden had been placed. The combination of digging the earth at the old gravesite and her highly elevated emotional state triggered the ability to see the children's ghosts. I left, still feeling unsettled and concerned that there might still be a problem.

Around three months later, the mother called again claiming that things had gotten steadily worse. The ghost children were gone but now she was being awakened with screaming. More disturbing for her was that some of her daughter's friends were calling saying they had seen her daughter in various places. Yet when they called to her, she would just disappear.

It, then, became clear that the woman's daughter had died and was most likely buried somewhere on the property. I called the police and they went out but could find nothing to warrant further investigation. Immediately my house was broken into and I started receiving more "Back off Bitch!" messages.

The woman's sister called to inform me that the woman's husband was blaming me for putting crazy ideas into his wife's head and that I needed to be careful. She told me he had threatened her, and she suspected he had also harmed her niece.

Shortly after, the husband announced that he could not live with such a crazy, hysterical woman who did not trust in him. He left, sending her a divorce decree from Las Vegas.

Four years later I received a call from a police detective looking for the previous residents. The body of an 18-year-old woman had been found buried in an adjacent lot. The grave was directly behind the playground of the ghost children. The police had determined that the body had been there for approximately 5 years. Apparently, one of the officers had remembered my involvement, at the time the girl had disappeared, and hoped I was still in touch with the family.

As the threatening messages ceased when the stepfather left town, I was confident that he had been my stalker. Since that incident, I have been careful of how I handle the safety of everyone participating in a paranormal investigation. For this, I am truly grateful because, in The Case of the Hidden Tunnel, had I not been so careful, I definitely would have woken up dead, and most likely as a ghost.

I strongly recommend that when you go out on an investigation, you go out with a trained team or a partner. There are many amateurs that may want to join you, but unless you know that they are qualified, they may leave you with a legal liability. Just because someone has watched every paranormal series on TV doesn't make them qualified. I've watched every FBI and CSI episode I could find, but I doubt that I'd be allowed on a crime scene. Anyway, you don't want someone who will antagonize the ghost or the client. You want someone who will have your back and add to the professionalism of your investigation.

It is not necessary to go out at night or to investigate in the dark. People are home on weekends, and business takes place during the day, so you are bound to run into a ghost at any hour that you visit the premise. Yes, a few techies prefer the dark, but, first, go out during the daylight to determine what you are dealing with. If something needs further investigation, you can come back in the dark. Since you have already scoped out the property, you will be aware of anything potentially harmful. Daylight investigations are easier because you are less likely to traumatize your client or yourself. There is something about movement in the dark that puts us all in survival mode and causes us to overreact. Remember that your job as the professional is to reassure the client, not add to the terror.

Be on the alert for safety hazards: cracked cement, tipsy book cases, broken stairs, missing rails, objects in the passageways, nails and screws. Notice if a surface is slippery or if a rail pulls away from the wall. I was on the third floor when I leaned on a rail to see below and suddenly found myself stretched out over the patio beneath. Had my investigation partner not put a belt around my waist and pulled me back, I most likely would have become a ghost. Test, and proceed cautiously in any unknown environment. I've got bruises and scrapes to prove that investigations can be physically challenging.

Also, remember that animals get protective of their property and their family. When the family gets nervous and reactive, the mildest of dog can become aggressive. I once had a parrot fly to my shoulder and rip my earring out, leaving me drenched in my own blood. Meanwhile, the owner agonized that the bird would surely die if he swallowed the earring. As luck would have it, I found both the earring and the First Aid Kit.

I consistently ask owners to lock up their pets, when at all possible, or, at least, have them supervised. I fell over a cat once and could have fallen down the stairs, but, I'm happy to report that the handrail held.

Walkie talkies are a great tool for paranormal investigators because you can have a fast response from another team member. In fact, that team member may arrive in time to video record the entire situation. Then you can totally figure out what happened.

Lastly, all paranormal investigators need to pay special attention to debunkers, set-ups and potential hoaxes. It is rare, but it has happened to me. Once I had a client's husband make weird noises and turn the lights on and off throughout the entire investigation, in order to prove I was a fraud. I merely told him that the theatrics were distracting. It turned out that the problem was not with a ghost. Rather, their problem was with loose plumbing.

Another time, a client threw incriminating evidence in the bed of my truck. It's a good practice to lock your vehicle, and only bring in any items you are using on the investigation. Keep all your possessions with you, otherwise, if some of your spendy equipment disappears, the client may insist that the "ghost took it—it steals everything!"

V. Investigative Equipment

Every professional Paranormal Investigator should have a few gizmos and gadgets, as there is nothing more exciting than flashing lights and whistles. For those of us that are intuitive, it's a wonderful validation when others can also see something happening, while the techies are able to corroborate it with one of their little magic boxes.

Ah, and then, the skeptic! If I have someone who needs proof, I hand them a few meters and leave them to experiment. Often, when I collect the equipment, I get some of the best stories, as well as the satisfaction that this individual was fully entertained.

Technical equipment gives an abstract form of validation to what can appear as a rather surreal experience. Imagine a psychic coming into a client's residence, walking room to room, maybe having a conversation with the air, and then issuing the statement, "Yes, there's a ghost in your house!" Not too convincing. However, throw in an assistant with the EMF meter, set up a Rem-Pod, and after a few bells, whistles and flashing lights, not only is everyone having a sensational time, but they're believers.

Now, I'm in no way saying that we should mislead the property owner. They most likely called you out in the first place, so they are aware that something is happening. However, the field of paranormal investigation is sensational, so let's have a little action!

I don't recommend you go out and purchase every piece of technology you find. Rather, go out with a few seasoned professionals and see what they recommend. Often, they will lend you the equipment and you can get a feel for it. Then get busy and do some research, and remember to read consumer comments, as you'll soon discover what works and what is less than effective.

Here's my recommended list:

Backpack or bag - Have something to haul your equipment, even a rolling suitcase will work.

- Make sure you can get everything into it.
- Have an individual mini-bag for each piece of equipment. This will protect each item and will help you be certain that you have collected everything when you are ready to leave. Or you can also buy a piece of foam and cut out a space for each item. This keeps everything padded and also serves as a reminder of what pieces you have loaned out.
- Make sure it is easy to carry and keep it with you or in your locked vehicle. Much of this equipment is expensive and you don't need it getting tripped over or disappearing.
- I often ask the client to place any equipment he's borrowed during the investigation back inside the bag. This way he can feel confident that I'm not pilfering any of the silver.

First Aid Kit - Keep it restocked and include medical information on each team member. For privacy, you can have each team member fill out a medical information form and put it in a sealed envelope only to be opened in a medical emergency.

Team Badges and/or Uniform - This is your image, so make a positive statement. Whether you have everyone wear a black or grey shirt, matching vests, or a pink boa, it's up to you and your team. Personally, I have my eye out for a red boa. If someone is prone to play drama queen, I think he should be identified up front. Give the client a definite way to identify who's with you and who's not. If the client has been telling everyone that they're having a paranormal investigation at their house, you can't always control who shows up. I once had a complete stranger wandering around the house. I thought they were a guest of the owner, and she thought they were part of the team. Introduce everyone before you start and make sure the client knows how to identify your team even if you buy a pack of stick on badges.

I recommend that if you pay money for fancy badges, you store them in the backpack after the investigation. There's always at least one team member who will forget his badge. Also, when you order the badges, get a couple of extra with just the team name so that if one is lost, or you have a new member, you've got a badge to lend until you get a new one made.

Flash light - There are always attics, crawl spaces, basements and areas where there are no lights; so be prepared! If you're going at night, invest in a high-powered flashlight and bring a dump truck load of batteries.

Clipboard

- If it's in your hands it will guarantee that you record information as you go, this way, you don't forget something of importance later.
- Also, having your hands full makes it obvious that you are not pilfering the silver.
- Ah! And most importantly, it gives you a strong surface to clutch when you are inclined to scream frantically and thrash your arms about.

Painter's tape - This will allow you to mark a location without damaging the walls or flooring so you and other team members can go back and do further studies. In a larger property this is so much easier than trying to describe a particular spot on the telephone or walkie-talkie, and so much simpler than having to run back and forth to point things out to another team member.

Batteries! - Lots and lots and lots of batteries for all your equipment. It's frustrating how quickly they drain when there's paranormal activity.

Trigger or Control Objects - familiar objects that children might be tempted to play with or adults commonly use.

Sense of Humor - remember to keep your wits about you.

Olympus WS-821 Digital Recorder - If you ever find this specific recorder at a garage sale or pawn shop, snatch it up! It's one of the best ever made. Most digital recorder work okay, you just need to try them out to find the one you prefer. Hopefully there will be some new equipment specifically produced for paranormal investigation in the future.

Compass - A compass works by responding to the magnetic pull of the North Pole. Should it no longer point north, it is being influenced by another magnetic field. Just remember that electrical current has also been proven to cause a magnetic field.

EVP - (Electronic Voice Phenomena) - It's great for someone on the team to have a recording device. Remember,
unless everyone is quiet, it can be a waste of time. It's good to
put up an orange flag to signal to everyone that a recording
is taking place. Electronic voice phenomena are electronically captured sounds that seem to resemble speech, but
are reportedly not the result of intentional recording. EVP
are commonly found in recordings with static, stray radio
transmissions, and background noise. Usually, EVP sounds
are short, only a word or two. The idea behind using an EVP
recorder is to record sounds at a frequency and pitch that
your natural ears are not able to pick up. Most paranormal
investigators assume that EVPs are communication from
entities existing beyond the physical realm of existence.

- **Analyzing Your EVP Recordings for Free** Once you
  have your digital voice recording file downloaded to
  your computer you can analyze the EVP with free
  software from Audacity or Wave Pad. It will filter
  out background noise and help you better analyze
  your EVP's.

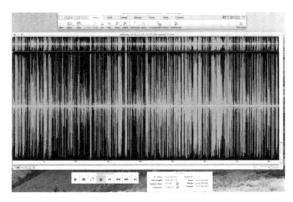

http://www.nch.com.au/wavepad

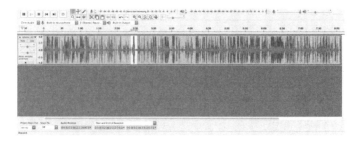

http://download.cnet.com/Audacity

EMF - (Electromagnetic Frequency Meter) this can also alert you to excess electrical voltage. I personally have found that old homes with the knob and tube wiring will consistently register areas of high electromagnetic energy. Make sure you determine where the electrical panel and other electrical appliances and lights are located before you get too excited about these readings.

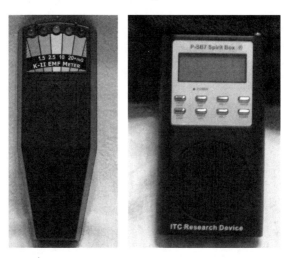

K-2 Meter and P-SB7 Spirit Box

Due to the theory that "ghostly" manifestations cause a disruption in the ambient electromagnetic field, investigators have incorporated a wide array of EMF (electromagnetic field) meters as part of their standard equipment.

An EMF meter must be in the EM field of an anomaly before it registers. The more sensitive the meter the further away from the anomaly it can register a reading.

The EMF meter measures electromagnetic emissions from anything that creates energy. Emissions can be given off by such things as appliances, animals, power lines, etc. However, most EMF meters are designed to ignore these readings and focus on the erratic and fluctuating patterns that are associated with paranormal activity.

How to use the EMF Meter:

All spirit entities or ghosts give off energy emissions. This energy creates a disruption in the EMF field allowing the EMF meter to detect their presence.

The meter must actually make contact with the ghost in order to register. So, follow steps below to make this happen.

- Gently scan the area you are investigating with a swaying motion from side to side as well as up and down. Never jerk the meter into position. Note: The Trifield Natural EM meter is especially sensitive to movement.
- EMF meters are also sensitive to power sources and will register such things as televisions, stereos, power lines or even a camera when it's too close to the meter. Always be aware of your surroundings before yelling,

"GHOST!" (The Trifield natural EM meter however, seems to be an exception to this rule and will ignore power sources.)

- Spirit phenomena will normally register in the range of 2.0 to 7.0 mill gauss. Remember to eliminate all power sources. Note: For those with Trifield natural EM meters, use the SUM setting for detecting ghosts.
- Try out your meter and become familiar with it before taking it out on a ghost hunt. Walk up to your television, stereo etc. and get a feel for how it reacts to these electrical sources. Check when they are on and when they are off for comparison.
- When scanning a room, be sure and check the furniture. This should include such things as the bed, the couch and the chairs. That's right, ghosts do relax. The same applies outdoors.
- It's best to have one person scanning with a meter while another is close by with a camera. When something is detected, the camera person can be notified and pictures immediately taken.
- Be sure and mark active areas with bright colored tape. Do this so that you can recheck these areas later in the investigation. This is done for two reasons.
  » Areas that register activity are usually frequented by ghosts and should be considered a hot spot for your studies.
  » It is also important to recheck these areas in case it's just an electrical reading. If continued checks reveal high readings, then it's most likely electrically related.

REM Pod EMF Detector - Great flashing colored lights and startling sounds; this is a must have when dealing with the skeptics. A small telescopic antenna radiates a magnetic field around the instrument. This electromagnetic field can be easily influenced by anything that conducts electricity. Based on proximity, strength and EM field distortion, the four colored LED lights can be activated to signal any changes in this field. A rise of ambient temperature causes a high pitch alert sound and a red light. When the temperature drops, a blue LED light visibly flashes and a lower tone is produced. This makes it possible to monitor the unit without having to watch it over long periods of time.

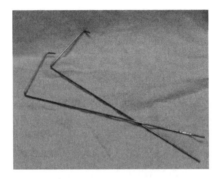

Dowsing Rods- Dowsing is a method in which a special device called a divining rod is used to locate water, minerals, gravesites and other underground material. The traditional divining rod consists of a long, forked stick which is lightly held by the divided ends and the elongated end is pointed parallel to the ground. The rod moves downward or upward independently when the person walks directly over the ground where water or other material is present.

It is theorized that dowsing tools are merely a way to extend the human response and amplify the natural intuitive signals so they become clear to the dowser. Dowsing is so popular that there are actually different clubs and societies throughout the world. One of the most noteworthy is the *British Society of Dowsers*, founded in 1933 in the UK which exists to encourage the study and enhance the knowledge of dowsing.

- **V Rod:** Traditionally made from a forked branch, this instrument can be made from any material such as wood, plastic or metal; most popular is a wire coat hanger.
- **Angle Rods:** These are L shaped rods, usually used in pairs. The shorter arm of the L is held in the closed palm with the long section parallel to the ground.

When the object of the investigation is passed over, the rods will cross over the spot.

- **Wand:** This is a single long rod held in the dominant hand that reacts with circular or oscillating movement.
- **Pendulum:** A bob on twine reacts with a number of different movements and is often used in conjunction with charts or a map for distant dowsing.

Laser Grid Pen- This high-powered laser emits a grid of green dots useful for detecting shadows or general visual disturbances during an investigation. Set it in front of a running camera to catch potential evidence. You can adjust the size and shape of the stars.

Cameras - this is mostly a personal choice. Some investigators like digital, others like the old fashion film in the camera. It's good to take one or two photos and see if orbs or other phenomena show up. Cameras are great at catching movement, forms, lights, mist and also orbs. Just remember, not every orb is a spiritual phenomena; dust and rain in the air can cause orbs as well. Notice if the orb is drifting, or disappears from one frame and reappears in another. Does it stay in the same position? Can you see a face or a form when you enlarge the orb? With time and experience you will be able to determine whether there is spiritual activity or whether your property owner needs a little more industrial strength housekeeping. Pictures make a nice addition to your report, so spice it up.

SCD-1 for Windows and the SCD-2 - These ghost boxes scan the internet radio in real time allowing ghosts to pick specific words in order to send messages.

Echovox Android App (Spirit-Box Radio) - The question arises, can non-physical beings use acoustic resonance to manipulate sound waves to communicate? Since spirits exist outside time and space they apparently have the ability to manipulate the audio on an energetic and vibrational level. The idea is that spirit grabs letters to form words to project into our reality time and space.

Walkie-Talkies - This is a must when exploring a large property such as hotels, factories or farms. The team can spread out and therefore have quiet and less interference, but if something happens everyone can be immediately alerted. It's also a good safety feature should someone have an accident; the person can immediately radio for assistance.

VI. DEVELOPING YOUR
INTUITION AND PSYCHIC SENSES

So where does psychic fit in? It's one of those "chicken or the egg" dilemmas. Which comes first: psychic development, or the ability to perceive beyond the physical into the nonphysical? Does having the spiritual connection create the psychic connection? I have noted that the more spiritual a person becomes, the more psychic abilities develop—and the more psychic the individual becomes, the more in touch she is with the Divine.

The label, "Psychic," comes complete with the understanding that the individual so titled is certified as crazy, or in the very least, eccentric. Now, "psychic," by dictionary definition, pertains to phenomena that are gathered by extrasensory or mental telepathy, and are not explainable by natural laws.

So, let me break this down: "Psychic" is really a catch word for awareness that doesn't conform to scientific understanding. That takes in a large group of perceptions, including physical abilities that have not yet been fully researched and spiritual gifts that may not be physically proven.

Hmm!

To be "psychic" is to be able to access information from the spiritual realms. The major problems are consistency and accuracy of interpretation, as most intuitive information is received in fragmented and symbolic form. It is normally just a glimpse here or there, or a feeling, which may include a probable outcome.

It is important to remember we all have freedom of choice. Thus, each choice that we make shifts the potential outcome. I tell my clients that my gift makes me a navigator, which allows me to point out where they have been and where their actions are leading them. If they wish to change the outcome, they merely need to make choices that lead them towards another goal. An example might be seeing the client's parked car rolling down a hill and smashing into a police vehicle. Ooops!

Being so pre-warned, the client now has a variety of choices: don't park on the hill, take the bus, get the brakes repaired, place blocks behind the tires, etc. So, it becomes a matter of choice. Now, the interesting dilemma is that by changing anything, everything changes, and there is now no way to validate whether the original information was correct. Yet, I still have individuals who report that they didn't change anything and indeed they had problems with the car brakes or the car rolling. As my goal is to help others, I'd rather someone proves me wrong by the choices he makes, than that he suffers needlessly.

What of self-fulfilling prophecy? Once a person has received an idea, does not that very suggestion influence his decisions on a subconscious level? For the most part, I avoid fortune telling. I use my abilities to take the moment and overview the situations in an individual's life, point out patterns that may be self-defeating, and then offer strategies and skills for success. My philosophy is that psychic information should be provided to help individuals become more responsible for their lives. If my instincts tell me that the information will only traumatize an individual, I move on to more instructive information.

There are a lot of misconceptions about being psychic. I can only write from my own experiences because psychic aptitudes are different with everyone. Much of what is portrayed about being psychic is merely fantasy. Psychics are believed to read minds as well as the future. This is not true. Psychics can see patterns that lead to probable outcomes. With skill, we can operate as navigators to give an individual guidance. It is important to remember that each individual has freedom of choice, and the insights of a psychic are just that. I have not as yet met anyone who had the ability to read a mind or know every detail of another's life.

Psychics are seen as having special powers that come from a negative source. This is not true. Whereas these abilities may appear supernatural, almost everyone has them to some degree. I have found that most interested individuals can develop their psychic abilities with time and practice. Most people speak about following their hunches, gut reactions and instincts, but seldom do they perceive this as psychic ability. As for being negative, it depends on the user. Most saints demonstrate varying psychic gifts.

To be "psychic" is to be hypersensitive on all levels. It is not always the most comfortable way to live. Besides being spiritually sensitive, many psychics have physical, emotional and mental sensitivities. Smoke and perfume always trigger a negative response. Food and alcohol can create radical mood swings. This hypersensitivity can be so distracting that it is hard to remain focused at times. The stereotypical psychic, who seems to be in a trance, is not far from the mark when an intuitive has not learned to manage the ability.

Being branded as a psychic is not always comfortable for me, so, I personally select my own labels. I use the term, "intuitive" to describe my psychic abilities. To be intuitive is to trust one's instincts. Most people are, at least, aware of their instincts and do not fear them. Therefore, people can relate to my psychic gifts without feeling vulnerable.

"Woo-Woo" is another silly term always accompanied with a rise of eyebrows and a quick glance to both the left and right (in that order) before continuing the sentence. This is not the sound a train makes. Rather, "woo-woo" is the wooing of one to the spiritual side. Therefore the statement, "He's into that Woo-Woo (the speaker's eyes rolled left, then right) stuff." This simply translates to "He's fascinated with the exploration of the unknowable spiritual realm." The eye movement is merely a futile attempt to glimpse into the subtle realms.

Honestly, there are many less than flattering terms for the paranormal and those who investigate it. But there was a day when people laughed and made fun of the idea that the world was round. Why shouldn't the uninformed also laugh and poke fun at the idea of the world being spiritual?

At this point I would like to mention that—whereas, we divide our world into what is seen and unseen, physical and spiritual—it's all one. I like to think of it this way: the spiritual realm is all around us. It literally envelops the physical realm. I like to compare it to the human body. The physical world resembles the heart and vascular system, and the spiritual world: the nervous system, all the other dimensions are lumped into a vague idea of other worlds. When we die, we are still here in the same reality, we are just transformed. We are no longer limited to the cardiovascular system; we are expanded into the whole multi-verse.

As I stated before, I feel most people are psychic to some degree or the other. But with a commitment to develop this ability, I have found my students begin to trust their intuition and start to gather information that is validated over time. The key word is trust. We all have hunches and feelings, but how do we learn to listen to them? In the same way we master a sport or learn to play music: practice, practice, practice.

I strongly recommend, if you are serious about developing your intuitive abilities, that you get yourself a fun psychic tool like Tarot, Numerology, Runes, etc. and just play. The more you can validate your hunches and read the signs and symbols, the quicker you will gain the confidence to trust your instincts. When you do a paranormal investigation, don't share any information until you have had a chance to process it. You will be amazed how much you naturally pick up on.

The following five exercises are necessary to train your mind and filter out reactive behaviors. They also contribute to a sense of calm and clarity. When we feel in control, we are much more likely to take the leap. Practice the following five exercises and you will find over time, your intuitive guesses become extremely accurate.

EXERCISE #1: RELAXATION

Make this exercise as physical as possible. Use exaggeration and visualization to intensify your experience. You are re-training your body to relax at will through a simple exercise of contrast and comparison.

- Assume a comfortable position that you will be able to maintain for an extended period of time.
- Work with your breath; by keeping your focus on it as you breathe in and out.

Use the inhale to maximize the tension of the muscle group you are focusing on. Think into the body: "tense" as you inhale and tighten your muscles. Always release with your exhale. Command your body to: "release" as you exhale and let the energy flow.

- Begin by tightening the muscles of your feet. Hold until your feet become hot and uncomfortable. With your next exhalation, release, allowing the energy to flow out through the soles of your feet.
- Next reposition your legs in order to optimize tightening the muscles of the ankles and calves. Hold, intensify, and then release. Let the energy flow down through your ankles releasing and clearing the energy as it drains out through the soles of your feet.
- Move your attention to the thighs. Hold, intensify and then release.

Work with your breath. With each release, remember to let the energy flow down through your thighs, your knees, your calves, your ankles and then out through the soles of your feet. The contrast of your muscles being taut and then relaxed will facilitate your body to release on a deeper level.

As you move the energy, thoughts and feelings may rise to the surface; just observe them as they flow out with the energy. Stored within the muscle is a memory of pain and other feelings. These emotions became trapped when we were tense and worried.

- Tighten your buttocks, hold, intensify and then release.
- Inhale sharply while sucking in your stomach. Pull it up and back, then hold, intensify and release.

- Tense the back pressing your shoulders downward as if carrying an excessive load. Hold, intensify, and draw in a deep breath. Shrug your shoulders as you exhale, letting the load slide from you as you send the energy down your back, into your buttocks, through your legs and out through your feet.

Identify the contrast between tense and release as you visualize the energy flowing down and out. Notice if your legs are tingling.

- Make fists, hold, and intensify. With the next exhalation quickly open your hands stretching them wide to allow the energy to flow out from your palms and finger tips.
- Raise your elbows tightening the muscles of your upper and lower arms. Hold until the arms begin to shake. Release, allowing the energy to flow out through splayed hands.
- Tense your shoulders again, this time raise them up to your ears. Hold, intensify and then release. Roll your shoulders back and then expand them open into a level position.
- Draw energy up across the back of your scalp and down into your face pulling your features into an exaggerated scowl. Hold the grimace, growl, and while you continue to hold, draw a deep breath in, then release. Let the energy wash over you as it flows through your body to release from both your hands and feet.
- Allow your jaw to slacken. Tip your head slightly back and feel you brain settle into your skull as your eyes warm and roll upwards in their sockets.

Take three slow deep breaths. As you exhale think into your body, "relax."

The most valuable way to relax is to give a verbal command to yourself to release. Stress is caused by the inability to let go. Most individuals respond effectively to verbal suggestions. Give yourself a self-releasing suggestion; "Let go!" "Relax!" You can pre-record your relaxation exercise if you prefer as hearing your own voice can draw you to a theta state of consciousness where you are more responsive to suggestions.

Soften your shoulders and allow your mind to quiet.

After you have worked with the above techniques for a period of time you will be able to accelerate the process and achieve the same results. Sit up straight in a comfortable position. Simply tense your entire body, hold, intensify, and then release. Allow the energy to flow over and through you as you command yourself to, "Let go, relax!"

EXERCISE #2: CENTERING

Centering is the physical, mental, emotional and spiritual act of coming to an inner balance. It is accomplished by finding the personal comfort zone which allows you to feel powerful and in charge of all levels of yourself.

One of the most necessary qualities required to develop spiritually and psychically, is a clear intention. In order to accomplish this, the body, mind and spirit must contribute to the sense of inner focus. Centering is a powerful tool in the journey to Self-Mastery which is necessary in order to build self-trust.

EXERCISE: Centering in the Mind

- Sit up straight in a comfortable position.
- Close your eyes.
- Begin by relaxing your entire body. (See EXERCISE: Relaxation)
- Clear your mind and emotions. I often visualize erasing a blackboard.
- Visualize a pattern gridded within your head. Mentally follow the lines to the center of the web. Observe yourself taking a firm grip and anchoring to this center point. (Anytime your attention wanders use the lines of the grid to pull yourself back to the center of your mind and re-anchor.)
- You are now centered in your mind.

EXERCISE: Centering in the Heart

- Follow the first four steps from above. (See EXERCISE: Centering in the Mind)
- Visualize a rose bud within your heart. Identify its color, shape and fragrance.
- Mentally see the rose open and expand until your focus rests in the center of the rose.
- See yourself sitting within the center of the flower. Smell the aroma. You may use perfume or other scents to facilitate the experience. (Anytime your attention wanders, bend over slightly and inhale. Imagine the petals of the rose surrounding you.)
- You are now centered in your heart.

EXERCISE: ADVANCED CENTERING

- Sit up straight in a comfortable position
- Close your eyes.
- Begin by relaxing your entire body. (See EXERCISE: Relaxation)
- Clear your mind and emotions.
- Breathe in, drawing energy from the Universe into the top of your head through the Crown Chakra.
- Continue to direct this energy down your spine into your tailbone or Base Chakra.
- Breathe out, sending energy from the tip of your spine or Base Chakra up your spine and out through your Crown Chakra.
- Pull yourself inwards towards your spine as you continue to breath in and out, receiving and sending energy.
- Become the energy you are breathing
- You are now centered within yourself

EXERCISE #3: GROUNDING

- Close your eyes and become focused on your breath allowing it to flow in and out in a relaxed repetitive pattern.
- Begin by relaxing your entire body. (See EXERCISE: Relaxation)
- Clear your mind and emotions.
- Visualize yourself sitting in a chair on the earth; a bar of metal passing through the interior of the earth.
- Now visualize your tailbone extending down into the earth like a long straight tap root. See this prehensile tail wrapping around and securing you to the metal rod

at the center of the earth. Give it several strong tugs to establish that it is secure.

- Now, bring your attention back to the soles of your feet. See your feet planted in the thick earthy loam of the soil.

- Visualize energy running from the ground up through the soles of your feet filling your entire body with earth energy as if you are an empty container. Take the time and make the image detailed and complete. See energy filling your legs and moving upward into your head, flowing down your arms and into your fingers and finally overflowing from the top of your skull.

- Next, look up through your third eye and visualize light pouring down from the heavens above, make it as real as you can image. This light is a healing ray and will appear in whatever form and color is most beneficial. Some people prefer to draw in white or gold light claiming it has the highest frequency. I just allow whatever light is in my highest good to flow through in the individual moment. To me it often looks like a descending helix, blending many different colors. Other times it is like a magical rain, sparkling with golden or white light.

- See this light entering through your crown chakra and filling you up from the soles of your feet until it also cascades from the top of your head.

- As the Earth energies and the Cosmic light come into contact, you may hear a soft hissing sound as they respond to each other and expand into an effervescent loam.

- You are now grounded.

CONNECTING WITH OTHERS

At this point you may wish to connect with others around you without being influenced by their energy fields. Some individuals have a tendency to drain energy. We have all experienced people that wear us out just by being near. The thought of spending time with them requires that we prepare ourselves. Once you are grounded, you will be able to easily feel a clear sense of self and maintain your personal boundaries. Should you begin to feel weary, step out of the energy field of the other, clear and run your energy, and then re-ground. You will immediately notice an exceedingly compact feeling of being here and now. Energy expresses itself as musical frequency does. Therefore, if one person is off key, it can throw others off. Learn to re-attune to your personal frequency and strengthen your energy field. Once you have practiced this exercise by simply focusing on Earth and Cosmic energies simultaneously, you will instantly ground yourself.

GROUNDING OTHERS

Once you have learned to ground yourself quickly and efficiently you may enlarge your energy field to include others. Do this by, first, grounding yourself, and then by visualizing the energy field being extended to include the other person. This is extremely effective for harmonizing parents with children, teachers with students, as well as healers with patients.

EXERCISE #4: MEDITATION

"Be still, and know that I am God ..." Psalms 46:10

Prayer is talking to God; Meditation is listening. Meditation calms the mind and allows the spirit to speak while the soul reclaims life. Many students have asked me what I experience when I meditate. My answers never truly explain the experiences. I was taught to clear my mind and keep it silent. Therefore, it is only on the return to wakefulness that I perceive what I have experienced. Mostly, my answer is light, calm, and an awareness of life. At times, my experience is like falling forward and simultaneously being drawn back. There is this floating perception, where I feel formless, yet aware and focused—not on thoughts—but on presence. My consciousness is riveted around 'beingness', a sense of expanded awareness. Everything is surreal, with a sense that nothing has more importance than just "to be". It all makes sense, yet there is no true comprehension, just a transcended sense of knowing, like a Divine Order.

- Begin by being physically relaxed. (See EXERCISE: Relaxation)
- Clear your mind. It may help to visualize a feather duster brushing away all thoughts.
- Tell yourself that you intend to relax and clear your mind and do not want to be disturbed for the next 20 minutes (or other exact amount of time.)
- Clarify your intent and mentally command it into being.
- Keeping your eyes closed, focus on the Third Eye. This is the 6th Chakra located between the eyes on the brow ridge.

- It is helpful to breathe in through the nose and out through slightly parted lips. When you first begin it may be helpful to count the breaths. Breathe in to the count of four—hold for an additional four counts— breathe out to the count of four—hold to the count of four, then repeat. Once this breath becomes natural, just observe the breath flowing in and out.
- Allow yourself to just perceive without thinking about what you experience. It is like the moment just before you nod off to sleep when you are aware, but disconnected.
- Witness and experience. (Keep brushing away any thoughts.)
- Merge into the light and energy that surrounds you.
- Surrender to simply being.

When you end this exercise, you may continue to experience a floating detachment. This is normal; you are most likely experiencing a higher conscious state of awareness. Do not be concerned. Each night when we sleep, the Higher Conscious Mind leaves the body and goes into the Spiritual Realm. This is known as Astral Travel. Each morning the body is awakened by the Conscious Mind and reset into a logical focus. A good night's rest will make you feel refreshed and more grounded.

EXERCISE #5: BUBBLE UP

Many naturally gifted psychics have empathy; the ability to accurately know what another individual is feeling. I believe that emotions from other individuals register directly onto the nervous system of someone who has this empathic type of sensitivity. If I have not shielded myself, I will cry when someone thinks of a tragic loss. I respond as if these are my feelings even though I know they are not. This is exceptionally overwhelming for empathic people that do not realize that they have this gift.

I remember going to a football game and sitting between two people cheering for opposite sides. I screamed myself hoarse, and both of my friends were upset with me, because I didn't take the game serious enough to choose a side. Afterwards I felt so emotionally drained that I seldom go to a game unless I sit smack dab in the center of the fans on one team. I'm amazed at how enthusiastic I become about the game.

The practice of Bubble-Up allows me to continue to be aware of another's feelings without be overwhelmed by them.

- Think of someone you love.
- Expand the feeling out of your heart until it forms a large bubble.
- See the bubble as a large oval that completely encloses all of you.

Now you will be aware of what others are feeling in a more objective way. If someone directs strong emotion towards you such as anger, rage or inappropriate sexuality, you will observe this without feeling impacted by it. When their energy touches the bubble, they will not feel shut out, because the bubble will reflect the feeling of love back to them.

Signs of being an Empath:

1. Certain people can emotionally and physically drain you

2. You avoid confrontation, and if you try to stand up to someone else, you see things from his point of view and feel inadequate in voicing your concerns

3. Sometimes you think you heard someone, but they did not speak out loud

4. You immediately take on the symptoms of your sick friends and family

5. You get excited or depressed over things to which you are mostly indifferent

6. You feel strong reactions to people you have never met before

7. Nature revitalizes you.

8. You avoid crowds

9. There is a "ring of truth" to honest statements and a feeling of discord when someone lies.

VII. The Initial Interview

It starts the same each time—someone calls reporting a paranormal incident and his immediate conclusion is that it is a ghost. So, I begin.

Being a Ghost Buster is not as action-packed as rocketing out in the old Ghost Mobile and traipsing around with gismos and gadgets, attempting to catch a cloudy version of the Michelin Tire Man. It is an investigation. It begins by gathering the facts, then viewing the location. Yet, whenever I'm off to a true paranormal investigation, I get charged up. I plug in my now ancient copy of the *Ghost Buster's* song track and cruise down the road, singing at the top of my lungs as I head for my next grand adventure. Whereas I always try to keep it all low key with the public so as to defuse the fear and give credibility to my work, for me, paranormal investigation is truly an exhilarating experience. It's a hoot! Though, I must say, I am always sorely tempted to rumble up in a Ghost Mobile, dressed in a terminator suit, brandishing a cross, a Bible and a ferret cage, and yell "Out, damn spot, out!" That is my more theatrical side and I know, while it would be funny at the time, it would most likely create some great irresolvable trauma for someone—most likely, myself.

Normally I meet the client at a neutral place like a restaurant or coffee shop to hear his side of the story. I do this for a number of reasons. Most times, the disturbances are caused by more than a ghost. This initial encounter gives me a chance to prepare for visiting the site, where I am likely to find a number of different situations. Often there is a dimensional energy flow, known as a vortex, that can draw in a number of different spiritual beings. Vortexes also have a source of energy that feed poltergeist activity. There can also be negative thought forms and living occupants who are contributing to the situation. If I suspect that there may be emotional or physiological problems with a family member, I definitely want a qualified specialist on my investigation team. If there is a spirit that has attached to the client, it will normally accompany him to the interview and I can arrange to clear this entity attachment before I visit the premise.

Probably the best way to guarantee your safety, and that of your team, is to know what you are getting into *before* you arrive on the premise. Taking the time to sit down with the client in a public setting to gather the facts and make an assessment will save you hours of time and frustration. Let's face it, if you're unprepared, you'll waste time waiting on supplies or you'll have to reschedule. Worse, you could find yourself trapped inside someone's house and realize that he has a major mental health problem or a vendetta against psychics.

Once, I showed up on a property and was just entering the garage, when the factual owner showed up. The client, who contacted me, headed for the hills and I was left looking like a trespasser. My Initial Interview write-up gave credibility to my claim that I was there on a client's request to investigate. We were able to determine that the other party had lived on the property over seven years earlier. The current owner showed me around, but he made it brief and was definitely skeptical. Needless to say, I now ask people if they have the legal right to be on the property.

After you have become a seasoned investigator, what seems exhilarating for a client is normal for you, and to spend an excess of three hours hearing a recount of every little incident can become very wearing. If you have met with the client prior, and asked him to give you an overview of events, you can explain that during the investigation you need quiet because you are recording. Most clients will be happy to just observe. You can tell the client that if they think of something else before, or during, the investigation it would help if they just wrote it down.

The Initial Interview gives you the ability to establish not only your credibility but also ground rules about how things will be conducted once you arrive on the property. Once you show up at the location is not the best time to realize that you have totally no control of the situation. So, establishing with the client beforehand what is required is essential.

Normally, I invite one member of my team to the Initial Interview and tell the client they can bring anyone they want, as this helps me determine if I need to limit the participants. I once met a lady that had over 35 friends and family with her. Can you imagine how challenging it would have been to arrive at the premise and have to sort that out?

I didn't want the liability if anything had come up missing or broken, so I assigned a guest to each team member and, therefore, restricted the number of guests in the house to no more than five at any given time. They had to be quiet, because we were recording, of course. I believe over 40 people rotated through the house that day. Good thing we did an Initial Interview or we might have walked into a full-blown party.

There is no problem with proceeding directly to the property after the Initial Interview. If the location is difficult to find, this is often the best idea. However, since many of my team and the client often work regular hours, a large percentage of investigations are done on weekends. Thus, having already done the Initial Interview makes it easier to get on with the job.

Conducting the Initial Interview

- **Chose a neutral location** such as a restaurant or coffee bar to meet with your client
- **Establish any risk factors**
  - » Does the client appear credible?
  - » Does what he is reporting make sense?
  - » Is the property vacant?
  - » Does the client have a legal right to invite you onto the property? Tenant/Owner
  - » Is the building dangerous?
  - » Are there any hazards such as open well or stairs without hand rails?
- **Determine the type of phenomena:**
  - » Are there signs of a vortex?
    - Shimmering or sparkling lights
    - Unaccountable air flow
    - Strange music or sounds
    - Chronic ill health
    - Have objects disappeared and reappeared in same location over time
  - » Are there signs of poltergeist activity?
    - Are physical objects moved by the unseen?
    - Are there unusual stains on any surface?
    - Is there a teenager in the house?

- Is someone in the house involved in a new romance?
  - » Are there any signs of an entity attachment?
    - Is someone exhibiting changes in personality or behaviors?
    - Has someone become withdrawn or depressed?
  - » Are there signs of a Ghost?
    - Drop in temperature
    - A mist or shimmer appears repeatedly in the same area.
    - Smells and sounds such as perfume and singing, voices talking softly
    - The feeling of being watched
    - Reflections in mirrored surfaces.
    - Orbs that appear in the same location in all photographs

- **Have there been any recent deaths or loss in the family?**
- **Are there any skeptics or pranksters?**
- **Will counseling be required?**
- **Do you feel comfortable with the client?**
- **Are there any other concerns such as neighbors, family members, animals, etc.?**
- **Does anyone in the family have allergies?**
- **What does the client expect you to do for them?**

VORTEXES

I also need to arrive prepared as my intention is, whenever possible, to resolve the disturbance in a single visit. Should the phenomena be a gateway to another dimension, commonly referred to as a Vortex, I will need to either place a screen around it or physically shift it. I like to deal with this on my primary visit so I do not need to return.

HAUNTED, CURSED OR POSSESSED

Should the occurrences be created by the presence of a living individual, I must be sure they are present at the time I visit the location. Highly sexual and/or imbalanced individuals such as adolescents or those developing empathy, or experiencing a spiritual awakening, can actually create spiritual disturbances. These types of individuals often generate a form of electromagnetic energy that can give substance to pre-existing phenomena, causing it to be perceived. In the case of this type of poltergeist activity, the imbalanced rising hormonal activity of an adolescent can trigger spontaneous events where either a ghost or thought form materializes. This electromagnetic energy or ectoplasm, as it was once called, is Life Force or Chi Energy. In the case of poltergeist activity, this Chi Energy is actually animating thought forms, allowing them to have a small level of substance. In addition, this energy can seem to give more physical substance to a ghost, allowing it to have a more tangible effect. In an environment with little or no electromagnetic energy, a ghost may seem to pantomime actions, but add excessive electromagnetic energy and suddenly, a long dormant ghost can be seen and heard bumping and knocking around, and actually physically moving stuff. The lights may go off unexpectedly, the door may open or close, footsteps may be heard, a fire may start or a candle may be blown out. The ghost is merely continuing in patterns of daily living, but with access to electromagnetic energy, the apparition has more substance and can, therefore, physically affect the environment.

And, yes, there are also some people who are actually haunted, which is not to be confused with being cursed or being possessed. A person that is haunted may have a ghost companion of a family member, a friend or even a pet. Remember the ghost does not know it is dead so the ghosts of mothers and children, husbands and wives, employees, etc., will continue their daily routines which include interacting with living people. Remember, only a small percentage of individuals who die become ghosts. The good news is that the ghost will, on the death of the living companion, accompany her into the afterlife. As a result, it will no longer be a ghost.

I've assisted military veterans who have ghosts haunting them. Many commanders, who experienced the loss of members in their outfit, continue to have some of their soldiers follow them.

There also may be the case of mistaken identity whereas a baby or youngster who has died will connect with a maternal figure, most often, a mother who has lost a child. The child will often appear in photographs and wake the woman in the night.

A person who has been psychically attacked with negative thoughts, in other words, cursed, can through fear, expand this disruptive energy field. It is important to note that a curse can only be maintained when the recipient accepts that it is real. Fear and anxiety add to the energy field, allowing the negative energy to manifest in much the same way as a poltergeist. The best way to break a curse is to visualize the person that sent the negative thoughts and say, "I'm sorry that you were hurt. I forgive you. I love you."

Just as it is difficult to remain angry at someone who realizes they hurt you and wants to make amends, it is difficult to maintain a curse when someone greets it with compassion. It's important to stress here that negative attacks can only affect someone when that person reacts with superstition and fear. It is wise to answer every negative action with kindness or at the very least, disinterest. The more energy given to any emotion, the more it expands.

Possession happens where a disruptive spirit enters the body of a living person. It is extremely rare, as the will to be in control is predominately prevalent in all humans, but such phenomena occurs—only when a person deliberately abandons his body. Likewise, it ends immediately when that person decides to take back control. The only cases I have seen are where a person is addicted to drugs, such as meth or cocaine. Not all possessions are negative. The most apparent reason for possession is when there is abuse or mental illness and the individual no longer wishes to live. Sometimes Angels and Spirit Guides will temporarily step in when a person is suicidal or suffering, but once again, they must be intentionally invited in, and will leave when the person recovers.

There are rare accounts where an individual is recorded to have split or multiple personalities. This occurs mostly with individuals who are in extreme crisis and have gone into survival mode. I have often wondered if these individuals have invited in spiritual allies to help them function during a mental health issue.

PET GHOSTS

I will not waste my time if the client's intention is purely sensationalism. Some people actually love the idea of having a 'pet' ghost and are willing to pay to have a professional psychic confirm that it is, indeed, a ghost. Often, they may be seeking the history or the story line with no interest in freeing the ghost. They want to know the "who," the "what," the "where," and the "when," yet have no interest in the release. In fact, more than once, when I have asked someone in my Initial Interview why they want me to investigate, they have expressed that "owning a ghost" added value or novelty to their home. I just can't bring myself to legitimize a ghost for someone's personal possession. Such behavior puts an entirely new angle on "being possessed!" Eh?

Respect for the Living

I want to be respectful of the spiritual practices of all individuals involved. Somehow, praying to Jesus does not always have the same impact, when dealing with a Jewish household, as it does with a Christian household. Neither does a lot of superstitious "puff-and-stuff" go far to reassure a highly logical individual. Yet, those raised with ritual often need to *see* something being done in order to believe that the problem has been successfully resolved. So, at times, a little more theatrical display may be required. I'm a pretty down to earth person, but when it's called for, I can add a little flair to my work to assist someone in accepting that the issue has been resolved. Our beliefs do affect our reality, and if they are not taken into consideration, there is a higher probability of a recurrence of the incident. If the client doesn't believe the phenomenon has been cleared, he may keep the electromagnetic field emotionally charged with fear, thus, dragging in some new spooky housemate. Why does all this work if you're not going to completely end the problem?

Defusing the Emotional Impact

A pre-location intake can keep the investigation from blowing into an emotionally charged event! There is nothing quite as overwhelming as a group of spooked-up adults, traumatizing themselves. Hysteria and psychosis are not my specialties! Hearing the account beforehand helps to defuse the emotions and educate the superstitious. Most importantly, it allows everyone to truly feel heard. When I meet with the occupants, there is almost always one traumatized individual and one cynic. Should I not do an Initial Interview, it could be a potentially reactive, crazy-making affair. In such cases where I have not previously met with the clients, I find, when I first arrive, it can often be totally chaotic. Everyone is trying to tell me what has happened, dragging me here and there to point things out.

In addition, the one token skeptic will be glaring at me while looking for any opportunity to expose me as a fake. He honestly believes I am solely there to rip them off and upset the family. I always try to arrange a little hands-on ghost participation for the skeptic. Otherwise, years later, the non-believer is still lording it over the family—that everyone had a panic attack over a little loose plumbing, and the phony psychic was able to exploit their hysteria.

SKEPTICS

Once, I had a client's cynical husband follow me through his home, suggesting I was going to steal everything of value I could get my hands on, if he left me unattended. Insulting, but I find this a normal reaction from most skeptics. I just smiled at him and kept my hands on the clipboard. I invited him to stay with me, telling him I might need his help. He looked confused, as if I had suggested I wanted his assistance in stealing from his home. Dah! But, he stayed close.

I walked him into a vortex and stopped, so that he was standing directly within it. Then using copper pennies, which I placed in an arch around him, I began to shift the Vortex.

"Wow!" he shouted, as his eyes got big. "What was that?" Grabbing his stomach, he sprinted off to the bathroom. After that, he hung back and let me do my work.

Later, at the debriefing, he demanded that I explain what I'd done to him. I merely asked him if he truly believed I had the power to do something to him. I could tell he was unsure how to answer my question, particularly since his experience had been all too real. When I told him he was standing in a vortex into which I had driven a ghost, he lit right up.

"Really?" He was like a kid learning something really cool. His wife later informed me that he was telling everyone about how he got "slimed" by the ghost.

Quick Resolve

At the Initial Interview, once I have heard the client's input, I pinpoint hot spots to prevent a three-hour visit from becoming an all-day event. Once I know where to look, I can save time by not having to comb through the entire property or wait for an occurrence. I can go to these hot spots and, having a sense of what to expect, I check them out and quickly dissipate the problems.

From the Initial Interview, I am informed of the different type of activities that are occurring. Thus, before I leave the premise, I can check to see if I have fully cleared all phenomena. There is nothing more exasperating than getting home to find that the client is abandoning their house because the ghost was smarter than the investigator!

KEEPING THE ELEMENT OF SURPRISE

Also, in the rare event of there being a cognizant spirit on the premise, having the intake elscwhere prevents me from alerting the ghost to the plan. Conscious spirits, such as divas and other forms of Earth Spirits, may choose to hide, if forewarned. This makes it hard to detect them and often results in multiple visits. In other instances, these watchful sprits may be antagonized by the presence of someone, who they are aware has come to remove them. They may respond by creating chaos, slamming doors and flooding floors. This seldom is fun to clean up and definitely upsets the residents.

BUILDING CLIENT CONFIDENCE

Lastly, this primary meeting gives the client a chance to meet me and determine if they truly want me in their home. This consultation gives them some level of assurance about what to expect financially, as well as what activity will take place onsite.

It's not hard to imagine the concerns an already traumatized family might have. For all they know, I could turn out to be a true lunatic, running around their house, zapping the walls and furniture with ectoplasm or worse. I could attempt to seduce them out of their hard-won money. I might even antagonize the ghost and cause it to create a terrifying situation. What would infinitely be worse, would be to tell them that there was no ghost and that they need to see a mental health specialist. So, it's really important to establish some level of trust on both sides *before* I go out to the site of the disturbance.

Thought Field

Also, talking about the haunting outside the premise helps to prevent charging the thought field and emotional energies that poltergeists and other spirits feed on. Have you ever walked into a room where two people were experiencing a strong sexual connection? Or how about where someone was angry? If you have, you'll know what I mean by thought fields and emotional energies. These energies can remain within an area if not cleared.

When you physically bounce a ball, there is a vibration. There is also a vibration when you hold highly charged emotions such as joy, excitement, fear, anger, frustration or sadness. These vibrations will remain lodged within the environment until cleared or time dissipates them.

Concluding the Interview

So, after spending 30 minutes or so doing a basic information-gathering interview, I either set up a daytime appointment to visit the premise or I go home and email the client a letter making recommendations for the "real" problem. As a psychic, I have the ability to know if there is a ghost, a vortex, spiritual activities or "some game afoot" before I visit the premise. I always do a psychic reading when I take the initial call to determine how far I am willing to investigate. I'll go out for phenomena other than ghosts if the client truly needs help, especially when I know children are at risk.

My motto is: "Helping individuals help themselves" because I have found that if the client is not willing to assist in solving the problems, they eventually melt into a waste of time, and energy lost in reacting to a client driven trauma drama.

But, as I said before, I really have no interest in a setup designed to discredit the psychic. I can honestly say it's been tried more than once.

QUESTIONS TO ASK AT THE INITIAL INTERVIEW

- What types of phenomena have occurred?
- Who has witnessed these occurrences?
- Are these occurrences repetitive?
- Are these sightings increasing in frequency?
- How long have you lived/worked at this location?
- Who else lives/works at this location?
- Who is most concerned and why?
- Are there any children at the location?
- What are their ages?
- Are there any pets? Do they respond to the phenomena?
- What is the client's spiritual/religious background?
- What does the client want done about the phenomena?
- Does anyone at the location have mental or physical health issues?
- Does anyone at the location suffer from chronic depression?
- Why is the client seeking assistance at this time?
- What has recently changed that has caused the phenomena to be visible?
- Is the client afraid or emotionally distraught?

Teresa Carol

Property Address and Case ID

INFORMATION GATHERING REPORT

Investigative Assistants: _____

Client: _____ Cell: _____

E-Mail: _____

Participants _____

Family Members/Ages: _____

_____

_____

_____

Pets: _____

_____

Religion/Spiritual Preferences: _____

Ethnic Background: _____

Exterior Front _____

Exterior Right Side _____

Exterior Left Side _____

Exterior Back _____

Entry _____

Living Room
_____

Dining Room
_____

Kitchen
_____

Laundry Room
_____

Garage
_____

Family Room
_____

Den
_____

Stairs
_____

Master Bedroom
_____

Children Bedroom
_____

Other Bedroom
_____

Hallway
_____

Out Building
_____

I normally add the following footer to indicate the client, the location the date and the page number. I place my contact information here as well so it's easy for the client to find.

The Case of the Unbalanced Family - Client Last Name - County www.teresacarol.com (253) XXX-XXXX 4/12/13	1

VIII. Procedure

In *The Case of the Crying Infant*, the neighbors had reported the young mother to the apartment building superinten-dent, and later to Child Protective Services (CPS). They claimed that each night, for hours without end, a baby cried. No one comforted it; no one quieted it. The young mother was the only one in the building with a new baby, so they were sure it was hers. However, on investigation, CPS found that the young woman's baby was at Mary Bridge Children's Hospital in Tacoma, Washington. In fact, in the three months since its birth, it had never been home. The young woman's other young daughter was too old to sound like an infant and had been visiting a school friend when the baby was reported as crying ceaselessly through the night.

Sometimes the client who requests the clearing will not be the occupant as in *The Case of the Crying Infant*. The landlord had called me to clear the ghost because many of his tenants were threatening to vacate if the nightly crying did not cease. The young mother was hesitant, but agreed to co-operate because she had also heard the crying. She further claimed that she constantly smelled wood smoke, and heard a woman sobbing. Because the landlord was my client, I included him in the investigation. I needed to be extremely respectful of the young woman as this was highly intrusive of her home and her personal life.

In time, you will develop an efficient procedure that works well for you. But to begin, here are the basic steps that I recommend you take in any investigation.

1. **Scan the property for after images.**
   When I arrive at a premise, I stand in front of the property and examine the aura, or electromagnetic energy field that surrounds the structure. Often I can perceive grey outlines of other structures that no longer exist. Quite frequently I am able to confirm through a personal account or an old photograph that these other buildings did once actually exist and in fact at the exact location that the shadows appear.

   This type of after-imaging has been highly documented in a series of scientific studies using Kirlian photography. In a highly controlled experiment where all light was blocked, a specialized camera was used to take pictures of living and non-living objects. It was fascinating to see that all living things gave off a bright halo. The color, the density and the radiance of the light often changed under the influence of emotion. The most exciting phenomenon was that when part of a leaf was cut and set to the side, the halo still surrounded the entire leaf even though a portion was missing.

   I once participated in a study that included the use of a Kirlian camera. The experiment included photographing the hands of different psychics to see if individuals with intuitive abilities had different patterns to their auras. I was asked to place my hand on a film plate at the end of a long black sleeve. The sleeve was tied down and all of the lights were turned off in a windowless room. I was then instructed to concentrate on different feelings; love, hate; sadness, anger and even sex. When developed, each print, displayed different colors and different patterns, depending on the emotions. Love and sex had a glowing image, whereas anger and hate reflected a more shard-like pattern. The print for sadness was a deep misty gray which I thought was a misprint but the technician showed me similar prints of sadness from other participants and they all had the same misty quality. The research did prove that psychics have stronger and more sensitized auric fields. The final conclusion was that psychics are sensitive. Duh!

2. **Set up your technical equipment in predetermined hot spots.**
    When doing the Initial Interview it is important to determine where the client perceives the most activity. This is the best location to set up cameras, laser lights and a RemPod. If you set this up when you begin— in 20 minutes to an hour you can return and review your information—or if you're satisfied with your walk through, you can gather it up to review later. It's essential to note that as enjoyable as paranormal investigating can be, it is also time consuming and in order to have time to check out your recordings, you do need to limit the time on premise. Keep in mind, this may be fun for you, but the client already feels intruded on by whatever is causing the phenomena. So, be respectful and keep it on task. The average investigation, start to finish should run no more than three hours.

3. **Use the clipboard to record all impressions.**
    The clipboard is a fabulous tool in ghost hunting for several reasons. First and foremost, it allows me to write down my impressions immediately. The more

information I can record, the clearer my insight into what is truly happening. I'm not always willing to share everything I experience, and, by merely adjusting my position, I can continue to record data without anyone looking over my shoulder. Plus, with the clipboard, I don't have to try to remember later, or hunch over a table to have a flat surface on which to write. Some people like to voice record their impressions, but this can be difficult if another team member is recording or your client is standing with you.

Another reason that I use the clipboard is more or less the same reason I ask the client to accompany me, to give them confidence that I have not taken any of their property. Normally if there is a cynic in the family, they are the one I request to escort me so as to avoid unnecessary accusations. Having both my hands on the clipboard makes it obvious that I am not pilfering.

And occasionally when something really spooks me up, it's nice to have something to hold onto. A normal startled reaction is to jerk the hands up. Nothing like the professional Ghost Buster traumatizing everyone as she flails her hands around wildly. Many a time I've gripped the old board, gritted my teeth and just walked through an unpleasant area, stopping only when I'm through to make notes. It's interesting how many times this leaves the skeptic standing directly in the phenomena and I can normally see by their face that they *do* notice the shift of energy.

4. **Fill out the Investigation Form and draw a map.**
I have a standard form that I pass out to all partici-pants. It's quite simple and I update and add to it from time to time. Primarily it gives me a way to organize

the data and quickly gather it from the team. I often draw a map on the reverse, notating energy patterns, so I can get a better picture of what is happening. If there is an underground water flow it helps me decide how best to redirect it. It often allows me to determine the exact position of a vortex as it may be suspended in the air or halfway through a wall, ceiling or floor. Once I finish the walkthrough, I am able to go home and write a report, which I later email to the client. This provides a more concise idea of what I discovered and how I resolved any problems. It also lists specific tasks for the client to complete. I include my basic contact information and referrals of other service providers I feel can assist with any additional concerns. I think of this final report as a little souvenir by which to remember the now departed ghost. It also helps to legitimize any future ghost stories. Let's face it, almost everyone loves a good ghost story, and show and tell is so much more interesting with props.

5. **Gather Impressions.**
Next I move from room to room gathering impressions and recording them on the clipboard. I try to stay open and just let the information flow to me. Temperature, color and feelings are the most dominant impressions, but I may encounter a spirit, hear voices, and see strange lights or movements.

a) Temperature: There will often be areas that become remarkably chilly for no physical reason. These colder areas are a definite indication of spirit activity and can also represent underground water flows. Rarely there will be a hot spot; this is normally where a fire or an extreme act of violence occurred. Wading into a freezing room to stand scorched in a fiery center is a clear sign that a violent death took place on that location. Whenever there is a haunting, there will be definite areas where the physical temperature can be recorded as dramatically lower than other areas within the same building. Drafts or cold air movement indicates the movement of spiritual energy. Most likely this phenomenon is an indication of a ghost, but not always. I constantly check for the obvious, like an open window or vent. There is nothing that can discredit a paranormal investigator worse than not seeing what is apparent to everyone else.

b) Pay attention to odors, as perfume and flower scents are often strong where a woman has died. So many people report that they smell lilac or roses which were popular scent for women before the 1950's. And if you are old enough to remember dime store cologne, you will definitely react when you smell this at a haunted location. Likewise, motor oil, shoe polish, animal manure can be noticed around the work areas of a male ghost. And more than once the aroma of whiskey and beer lead me to discover a ghost who enjoyed his alcohol. I had one client that smelled fresh coffee every morning and fresh bread every Saturday.

c) Note any color impressions by looking around. I take in the colors that are physically present as well as scan the electromagnetic energy to see if any note-worthy colors appear. Areas can appear drab or colorless, and others spiked and splattered with reds, oranges, browns and on rare occasions green. The lack of color is definitely a sign that energy is being drained from the room. Fear, worry and continued depression can account for this type of phenomena and often appear in environments where someone with mental health issues lives. It can be from the ghost, but 90% of the time it is coming from someone currently living or working in the location. The more vibrant colors are indicative of uncontrolled passion or sudden surges of violence. In locations where a rape or other forms of violent attack has occurred, there will be large reddish-orange hued swatches of color. The more intense the color, the more premeditated and focused the violent act. Self-defense will appear orange with streaks of gray and clouds of confusion. Murder, especially premeditated, appears as brutal in color as it was in action. It is important to note that these colors can appear where there has been fighting, even though no one has died. So the energy fields of public bars and alleyways often have streaks of red, orange and brown. Cruel and sadistic individuals also may infuse their environment with strong, cutting, shards of color. Also, criminal activity such as drugs, guns and illegal money may be surrounded with a "red light" type of glow indicating the owner is fearful of being discovered. A deep rusty brown often exhibits itself in locations where someone who is criminally insane has been living. It's important not to confuse the fact that brown showing in the auric field of an individual represents connection with nature rather than mental imbalance. It is the splinters of color that has a vicious appearance that indicates the mental health issue more than the color. The shapes that the color takes indicate more clearly the intensity that they were created from.

Green trails of pulsing lights indicate the presence of Elementals such as woodland nymphs, fairies, divas, or even leprechauns, rarely seen in populated areas.

Remember to examine doors and other wood surfaces for patterns that show Earth Spirits maybe living in the woodwork. Knotholes that look like eyes, long tapered hands, or even silhouettes, can be an indicator that there was once a large forest here and the inhabitants have had to adjust to a different way of life. After I point this out to the property owner, I will suggest that a large tree such as cedar, fir or oak, be planted on the property so these Elementals can spend more time outside and hopefully have a tree to inhabit long after the building is gone.

6. **Touch into your feelings as you move through the location.**

I keep checking in on my feelings. In some rooms I may feel giddy and playful, while in others I will feel sad or tired. Such extremes may suggest someone who is taking medicine, drugs or could be experiencing other forms of mental instability. Still other locations will make me feel hostile and reactive or extremely paranoid. Normally these feelings are found where criminal activity has recently taken place. It is important to remember—whether these feelings belong to the ghost

or the resident—there is almost always a strong cor-
relation. Think of it this way, you have to share a like
vibration to be comfortable in such extreme energies.
A healthy person will not be comfortable living with an
alcoholic; likewise they will not be receptive to living
in a location where an alcoholic ghost lives. Thus, like
attracts like and there is normally someone in the residence with matching energy. In fact it may be their
energy and not that of the ghost that I pick up on.

7. **Pay attention to any physical pain.**
   One of the biggest indicators of how the ghost died
   is that the physical pain he experienced at the time of
   death can be felt on your nervous system. Notice if you
   feel like you're choking, hot, feverish, headachy, or experiencing chest pains. A sudden stab in the side can be
   a bullet or a knife wound, as likewise a feeling of being
   struck over the head maybe a falling object or something worse. When you write these symptoms down
   and return to find other team members experienced the
   same impressions, the picture begins to clarify.

8. **Listen for sounds and voices.**
   Voices will often speak, repeating the same thing over
   and over again. This might be a warning shouted in
   self-defense or someone calling for a person or a pet.
   This is a sure clue that there is a ghost as they often
   imprint their actions at the time of their death.

9. **Be aware of odd coincidences.**
   Once, in a single level home just off Pacific Avenue in
   Tacoma, Washington, I saw a large lavender orb rise up
   at an angle. It was followed by an audible shriek and

then the ball of light rolled down its original path and laid there until it faded away. Then, the entire event repeated. On investigation I discovered that a woman living in a two story house which had occupied the same location in around 1890 had fallen down the stairwell to her death. As she lived alone, it was a long time before she was discovered. She had died from injuries suffered from head trauma and a broken leg. Amazingly, almost everyone who entered the ranch style home built in the 1960's kept tripping over and falling down the entry steps. I did.

In almost every paranormal investigation, I am never sure beforehand what I will encounter. Sometime it is basic spirit activity such as changes in temperature, lights or colors, smells or fragrances, pronounced feelings or subtle mood shifts. Other times I will walk straight into the ghost or the environment in which the ghost lived. In these cases, I try not to scream.

When I am doing a walkthrough of a premise, I normally place myself in a semi-trance state so that I can pick up on the subtle energies. Sometimes this allows me to see through a dimensional doorway into the past to an emotionally charged moment. I believe that the stronger the emotion the easier it is to reconnect with the event. I am not sure whether this is through an energy imprint or through intuitive viewing. They are most likely one and the same.

I enter information into the top portion of the Paranormal Investigation Report at the Initial Interview and then I fill out the form in my computer and make copies for my team. Each team member may move around the premises in a different pattern. But when I go to correlate the information, it's easier if there is uniformity in reporting.

When I type up the final report I will include comments in each area from myself and my team. It's fun to lay out the forms and see, that whereas each team member entered the room at different times, so much of the information is the same.

I seldom share specifics from the initial walk through with the client until I can actually reach a conclusion and begin a plan of action. One of the most awkward moments I had was when a student humorously pointed out that the resident ghost was standing in the dryer and therefore, all the laundry would be covered with ectoplasm. Not funny! The home owner's sister showed up shortly and the client changed her clothing. Had that little tidbit not been proffered, we would not have taken a break for a wardrobe change. I am sure the lady of the house rewashed every article of clothing she owned after we left. She was sure that the ghost slime had caused a rash on her side. I don't think so; I noticed she was using a highly scented laundry detergent. Remember there is never any reason to distress people who are seeking assistance with spiritual phenomena. That's how false information can lead to the fear of the paranormal.

IX. What's What in the Paranormal

Well, if you've heard about it, it probably is out there somewhere. Just be cautious not to add to the superstition and fear. There are so many spirits that it is hard to identify even portions of them and where they reside. Yet for the sake of clarification I will use the standard Shamanic or basic tribal understanding of the spiritual realms; the Upper World, the Middle Earth and the Lower World.

The Upper World, also referred to as the Celestial Realms or Heavens, is the part of the spiritual world that is often perceived as the residence of God. The Angelic Hosts, the Faerie People, the stars of the Universes, Master Guides, Master Teachers and departed loved ones are believed to inhabit this part of the spiritual world. It is the highest realm, not in that it is superior to the other levels, but more, that it has the highest and most rapid vibration rate.

The Middle Earth is just that, our planet. The Earth is in the middle not because it is the center of the Universe, but because it is of a vibration rate which places it between the higher vibration of the Upper World and the denser vibration of the Lower World.

The spiritual inhabitants of the Middle World are numerous and vary widely. Besides human and animal spirits, there are the Earth or Elemental Spirits. These are spirits that are living, conscious qualities of the planet. They are also known as the elementals: Earth, Air, Fire, Water, Metal and Wood. They have been referred to as tree spirits, spirits of the wind, earth energies, water sprites, and so on. One famous Earth Spirit or Elemental is the volcanic spirit known as the Goddess Pele of Hawaii. Some of the forms elementals will take on are as Divas, Nymphs, or Sirens. They can be seen in a plant using a branch like a flag or causing a plant to bloom out of season. In locations that once had old growth forest, these spirits may migrate indoors to live in the wood of a building. Eyes, ears, mouths and small human-like bodies will appear in the grain of the wood if Earth spirits are living in a home. Should you observe phenomena, take a picture and date it. Come back in a few years and photograph the same wood surface and you will be astounded by the changes.

Then there are those we call the *Little People* who live in our Physical Realm. They are seldom seen because they have extreme rates of vibration, which make them harder to perceive. Trolls and Gnomes have dense earthy vibrations, whereas the Leprechauns, the Elves and the Faeries have light, airy vibrations. Most of these *Wee People* have migrated into our Physical Realm through vortexes or dimensional doorways. There are many legends of why they are here. Some, like the Leprechauns and Faeries have the ability to use the vortexes to pass between realities at will. In the past, many mythological creatures such as the dragon and the unicorn reportedly wandered into our reality and became trapped.

Twice I've come across a satyr-like being, known as a Breka that was protecting sacred ground. In each case the homeowner had seen it upon the roof and running away through the fields. One lady reported it opened her shower curtain, and then went out the bathroom window. I know this sounds a little farfetched, but amazingly we saw it on the far side of the pasture and when we returned to the car there were hoof prints of something larger than a goat that had walked over the top of our vehicle. It's important to keep an open mind. Record the facts and keep your cameras ready. You have a lifetime to figure it out.

Vortexes are a honeycomb of inter-dimensional portals or gateways which allow energy and sometimes matter to pass through to other dimensions. Energy flows through these interfaces much like the exchange points in the body where the blood exchanges air for carbon dioxide or food for waste products. To me they look like a shimmering or twirling light, much like looking at heat rising off the pavement, except vortexes can be more colorful and its energy flows in all directions. The vortexes are selective in that they either flow into or out of our reality. There are a few vortexes which have the ability to allow passage both ways but they are the exceptions. Most vortexes lead to either the Upper or Lower Worlds. And it is thought that some vortexes may actually connect locations within our physical world. I can see vortexes but I have found little information to explain them. As modern scientists continue to explore dimensions, I am hopeful that I'll gain a better understanding. Currently I refer to Wikipedia which gives some interesting facts: one being that the spout of a tornado is an example of the visible core of a vortex. They are dimensional doorways. This, I learned in my early days of investigation when I would pass through them to see where they went. Now I don't bother as it never helped me clear the paranormal phenomena. You can learn to do this as well by mastering either remote viewing or astral travel.

The Lower Worlds, not to be confused with Hades, is the densest vibration. Hades or Sheol more commonly known as Hell does reside within this lower vibrational plane, yet it takes in only a small area. Sheol is the fiery furnace referred to in the Bible for the purification of the immortal soul. Just as a furnace is used for separating impure materials from the precious metal, this furnace burns out the destructive behaviors that have polluted the soul. It is interesting to note that just as a jeweler is able to quickly separate out the different contaminants within the metal, so also is the soul quickly purged in the fires of Hell. The idea of burning eternally in Hell might be a great deterrent to the religious criminal; however, it is not realistic.

In the Lower World live the people of the Inner Earth and many other subterranean races such as the Gnomes and Trolls. Also, there is the City of the Demons which is darkly Gothic in appearance and is inhabited by milk-skinned, extremely gaunt people as well as their Demon companions.

It is important to mention that the Lower Worlds are not within the Earth nor are they beneath the world; they are part of this same reality but at a more concentrated vibration rate.

The Upper World, Middle Earth and the Lower World are all the same reality; they just function at different vibration rates. The best example I can give to explain these different vibration rates would be a super highway.

Imagine four lanes of northbound traffic. The far right lane would be the slow lane, or the slowest vibration lane. Here cars are entering and exiting. The two middle lanes move at a more moderate rate. In the extreme left lane, the fast lane, traffic flows rapidly; it often appears to zoom by.

Whereas, it is the same freeway that drivers in each of the different lanes experience varying situations because of the speeds they are going.

Those driving in the slow lane will be crowded by traffic entering or exiting the freeway. These drivers will be forced to either slow down or move over. They are aware of the right hand shoulder and situations along the side of the road; they may be able to view something that has occurred on a ramp or even a side street. Their focus will be on the traffic entering and exiting the freeway and the vehicles in the lane directly to their left. They will watch behind and around the vehicle, but their observation, because of their speed, will be primarily engaged with other vehicles of similar speed. It is highly unlikely that these drivers will see much of the oncoming traffic.

Those driving in the middle lanes will be focused on their lane and the cars on either side. Whereas, they will note vehicles accelerating and decelerating to merge into their lane and they will not be concerned with either of the shoulders or the oncoming or merging traffic.

Those driving in the fast lane, in addition to being focused on their lane and the traffic to their right, will also observe the median and the oncoming traffic. If the oncoming traffic is separated, they may observe activity on side streets that pass beside and under the freeway.

It would be possible for three drivers to have three different experiences at the same time. Should there be a semi-truck parked on the shoulder, a careless driver weaving in and out of traffic, an ambulance speeding through the underpass, a bonfire near the road, or an accident in the oncoming lane, not all of the drivers would see each of these events. So it is with the spiritual world, so much is happening we can only take in what is closest to us.

In other words, even though there appear to be different realities, it's all one reality even though it's too large to grasp in its totality. Thus, spiritual phenomena appear in all three levels. Yep! The Upper World, Middle Earth and Lower World all are inhabited by ghosts

Apparition is the general term used for any number of different types of spirits and nonphysical phenomena. An apparition may be viewed as a vapor-like mist, a ball of light, a translucent form. It may appear to move an object, ring a telephone or turn on and off electrical equipment such as a radio, computer, or hair dryer. Apparitions may be Nature or Earth spirits, individuals who have died, or even inter-dimensional beings. Apparitions can also be energies such as thought forms, emotional energies, vortexes, or the electromagnetic energy lines that circle the planet know as Ley Lines. Even a true ghost is considered an apparition.

Here are a few signs to help you figure it out. Don't limit yourself to these basics. The best way is to get out there and learn through the experience.

Ghosts - Individuals who have died but do not realize they are dead and continue in life as if nothing has changed. Ghosts normally appear in a specific area and can also haunt items.
- Drop in temperature
- A mist or shimmer appears repeatedly in the same area.
- Smells and sounds such as perfume and singing, voices talking softly
- The feeling of being watched
- Consistent time patterns such as every morning in the bathroom, evenings in the kitchen, weekend in the shop out back, etc.

- The sound of footsteps, chopping wood, items being dropped
- Reflections in mirrored surfaces.
- Orbs that appear in the same location in all photographs
- Feeling uncommon discomfort or pain such as a head-ache or chest pain.
- Animals will watch and often respond with familiarity.
- Individuals in the family will dream they are talking to someone else in the house

Poltergeist Activity - When there is an excess of Chi energy, such as with an adolescent who has begun sexual development or even honeymooners, a mischievous or angry spirit can use this energy to physically move things. Items may be tipped over or thrown. In extreme cases some-one in the home will report being pinched or having her hair pulled.
- Is there a teenager in the house?
- Have any of the occupants taken a new sexual partner?
- Are objects moved by the unseen?
- Are unusual stains appearing on any surfaces?

Vortexes - Natural occurring passages into other dimensions.
- A sensation of dizziness in one specific location.
- A feeling of wind or a breeze
- Chronic ill health that improves when away from the property.
- Change of temperature, often warmer, but can also be cooler
- Sparks of whirling light
- Sounds, as if they are coming through a tunnel or tube.
- Feeling like energy is building-up or being drawn-out
- Disorientation

- Items that are dropped in the location disappear and may reappear after years
- Distortion as if looking through a prism
- A bright light on a photograph which takes the shape of a comma. What's interesting, is that when enlarged, it looks like a small tunnel
- Cats may lay in the center of the vortex, especially if it's warm
- Dogs normally walk around
- Batteries are quickly drained
- Electronics often won't function
- Many people report feeling nauseous

Elementals or Earth Spirits - The spiritual wild life. Naturally existing spiritual elements of this planet.
- Pranks
- Often shiny or sparkly items disappear
- Plants flourish and bloom exceptionally
- Constant flooding or water issues in the case of water sprites
- Small unexpected fires in the case of fire elementals
- Images of eyes, mouths, and bodies that change in the grain of wooden objects.
- A pet cat will hiss at or attempt to catch an elemental.
- Birds may suddenly learn new words or names
- Dogs may appear skittish or overly cautious.
- Machinery that independently starts and stops

Entity Attachment - a soul who realizes that he is dead but has not passed on for a number of reasons. This soul chooses to pal around with someone they know or can relate to and it lives vicariously through this host person. This is not harmful but excessively draining and can be crazy for the individual and his family. (This is not a possession)

- Excess use of drugs and alcohol
- Severe and unusual episodes of depression
- Someone not feeling or thinking like their normal self
  - » Gentle people might become violent
  - » Aggressive individuals might become submissive.
  - » Boring people might become more interesting
  - » Happy people often seem subdued
- Craving foods that the person previously did not like
- Speaking a foreign language
- Thoughts may surface about people unknown to the person.
- Hearing a voice which tells the person what to do
- Wanting to sleep
- Having bizarre dreams
- The individual feels like he's living someone else's life and has their memories.
- Dogs and cats often will avoid this person or react aggressively.

Natural Phenomena - Please don't miss the obvious. Look for natural causes such as trees rubbing against the gutters, or old pipes rattling in the wall.

- Are there any shrubs or trees that are touching the building?
- When was the structure built?
- Older buildings do have a tendency to creak, so listen to the floor as you walk.
- Look for cracks in the foundation and walls which indicate that the foundation maybe settling.
- Is there sign of rodents, birds or other animals?

» Look for animal fur, feathers or scat around vents and behind boxes, especially in garages or storage areas.

» Check to see if boxes or walls show signs of an animal gnawing on them.

» Does it appear as if birds or raccoons have torn out the screens to the attic vents?

» Are there overhead power lines?

» Do the neighbors have machinery such as a pump that turns off and on?

Fraud - A fraud is when someone intentionally sets up a hoax in order to deceive others.

- Is someone intent on seeing or videotaping your reaction.
- Does someone try to bait you into validating their impression of the situation?
- Do you feel like you are being steered or manipulated?
- Are there clandestine looks and giggles as if there is a private joke?
- Do things seem a little staged or too perfect?
- Are you finding little of the activity that was reported in the Initial Interview?
- Does the client appear credible or as if he is making things up?

Possession - someone who, because of excessive self-medication or mental health issues has called in another entity to live through them.

- Extremely rare and therefore you may never encounter
- Person will obviously need professional help or restraint
- I strongly recommend if you encounter someone who you believe to be possessed, you find someone in a

religious or medical practice that is qualified to assist and leave the situation in his or her hands.

Demons - mostly a catchall phrase for sensationalists who enjoy inciting terror. A true demon lives in another realm and does not bother to visit our world. So if there's a demon, you are definitely out of your league as you are most likely dealing with a person who can trap them and transport them to this dimension. Whoever has that ability and that proclivity, I personally would rather not deal with! The chance of discovering a demon without journeying to their reality is almost impossible.

X. Cures and Closure

In more than 37 years—the number of years that I have been doing paranormal investigation—I have never encountered the same situation twice. Please use the Initial Interview to prepare, but go out with a completely open mind. If you treat all investigations the same, you will find what you expect. However, you will not necessarily resolve the issue. You will either have to go back or face the possibility that the client will perceive you as not being up to the job and move on to someone who is more capable. Think about it, you have probably been in a lot of restaurants, even some which served the same type of food, but once inside, and though they have similarities, they are totally different. Keep this in mind when you go out to investigate: No two investigations are ever identical.

Once I have a basic picture, I inform the client of what I have found and what action I intend to take. Then, I begin with relocating and screening all vortexes, releasing the ghosts, clearing the negativity, and creating an uplifting environment. Finally, I return to the client and do a debriefing. This is when I recap my experience and make recommendations. Some chores I may leave for the client, such as trimming trees and mending gutters. I may also demonstrate how to set up a protection grid and encourage the client to repeat the process in outbuildings or within the entire property boundaries. Occasionally, if the client is going through a spiritual awakening, I may recommend a book to read and give a little basic education to help him stay balanced. If there is a drug, alcohol or mental health problem, I make suggestions and leave the client with pamphlets and referrals. Mostly, I just work on encouraging him to rebuild the energy in a positive way. I do this by offering specific instructions that are listed later in this chapter.

So how do I build a clarification of what is happening? Experience!

Mostly I just read through my notes to see what patterns surface. This is the time to find a private place and sit down with the team and consult. Be careful that everything is kept low-key and that children or reactive clients are not listening. Please no dropping of ectoplasm bombs! Remember you came in to resolve the issue, not terrify the client. So, plan to finish up the job without a crisis.

Because of my psychic gifts I may have already seen the vortex or the ghosties. Because of my ability to perceive, I may notice the overmedication or the emotional imbalance of someone in the household. Because of the data gathered and the statements taken, the investigative part of my brain begins to synergize the information and comes to a reasonable conclusion.

You will find with time and practice that you will be able to pull it together easily. In the meantime, take your best guess and cover the basics. Begin by checking in with the client to ascertain that no one has severe allergies. If so, you can open all the windows and doors and do a light saging. Avoid burning the herbs in this individual's sleeping area. If everyone in the premise is okay with burning sage, then take your time and sage the area thoroughly. Next, screen any vortexes, release the ghosties, place a copper grid, and do a house blessing. This should cover most of it as long as there is nothing of concern on your list.

Regardless of whether you can see paranormal phenomena or not, the following cures are effective.

Relocating and Screening Vortexes

Have you ever observed that a light in one specific location continues to burn out? Have you seen a specific spot on a road with good visibility, a place where there are accidents constantly? Have you noted a particular off-ramp where cars always stall out? Yep, you got it! It's most likely a vortex.

Small vortexes can be moved slightly, but the larger they are, they must be screened—the only cure I know that is successful. Please don't cap them, by covering them with copper. I have found that when energy is trapped it will build up until it breaks through. I accidently blew up a magnificent fir tree that measured over 27 inches in diameter by restricting the flow of energy.

On hearing me speak about earth weaving, a process of interconnecting energy from different locations on the planet, an Elder Native American woman informed me I was giving people misinformation, and then proceeded to instruct me in the correct way. Being trained to honor my elders, I believed that she knew better than I. So following her instructions. I laid out a crystal grid around the base of a beautiful tall fir tree. That night my husband and I awoke to the sound of a loud crack. It was followed by the sound of splintering wood and the boom of a falling tree. The same tree I had put the grid around in daylight lay in ruin. The remaining stump was a fountain of exploding energy. When I took the crystal grid away, the phenomena dissipated.

The ancient gentleman from the tree removal showed me a crosscut from the tree and excitedly told me, he had never seen anything like it in his entire career as a logger. What he showed me was a lightning strike not from the exterior of the tree, but rather from the inside blasting outward. Not only did the old geezer charge me $1,000 to remove the tree, he also walked off with my evidence. Note to self: Document, document, document! But what's worse is that I destroyed a magnificent tree. Experience can be a harsh lesson. So here's the easy way to screen a vortex.

COPPER VORTEX SCREEN

Should the energy from a vortex be intrusive or create accidents on the property, it is recommended that a copper grid be placed between the vortex and all inhabited structures. Should the vortex be inside a home, try placing a plant or an animal bed on top. Most animals are okay with this form of energy, but if they don't like it, arrange the furniture so no one is sitting in or walking through it.

Another technique is weaving a copper wire into a throw rug and laying it along one side of the vortex. I highly recommend that you don't restrict the energy flow by placing a copper planter or a copper table directly over the vortex. If you do, I'd be interested in your experience, but don't say I didn't warn you.

Begin by collecting a handful of copper pennies, copper wire or copper pieces. I keep a pretty pot near my desk that I toss my pennies into so that I always have a good supply. If you know beforehand that you will be doing grid work, ask your client to gather as many as he can, in order to have a sufficient supply available when you come to the premise. Remember modern pennies have little copper in them so you'll need pennies minted before 1982. After that year, according to Wikipedia, the amount of copper in pennies was reduced from 95% to 2.5%.

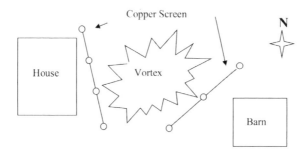

Lay the copper objects approximately 6 feet apart in a straight line (see illustrations above). The copper will form a barrier that will deflect energy. This will channel energy from the vortex away from the area you have screened, but it will not restrict the natural flow.

Using a Copper Grid to Stabilize Energies:

This is the standard protection grid, sometimes referred to as a ward. It keeps a dedicated energy flowing within set boundaries and screens out unwanted influences. I recommend this grid when there are disruptive outside energies, such as unfriendly neighbors, excessive overhead air traffic, power lines, industrial areas, high traffic flow, high crime area, etc. Putting a grid around a property will push out negative energies and allow the property owner to create a sacred space. At the same time it acts as a vibration that filters out energies that do not harmonize with the property.

As an electrician once pointed out to me, in order for energy to be managed, there needs to be three elements, a

positive, a negative and a ground. It is important to understand that if you create a center hub of positive energy, it
will be quickly encircled by negative energy. Thus you will
also need to project spokes of positive energy out into the
neighborhood and further on out into the community.

I once was invited into a shopping mall to help remedy
a problem with poltergeist energy. What I discovered was
that someone had preformed a powerful blessing at a
Christian book store located within the row of shops. The
book store had become a hub in the center of a hurricane
of negative energy. Once I began pushing lines of positive
energy from the store through the negative energy and
anchoring them into the community, there was an amazing
result. The disruption subsided, the local crime reduced and
the popularity of the shopping center skyrocketed.

Take a moment once the grid is complete and visualize
positive energy flowing out from the edges of the grid into
the neighboring properties, and out into the community
as a whole. I often go as far as seeing these trails of energy
migrating through the state into the entire North American
continent and on throughout the world. It maybe a little
excessive, but, I really don't want to re-do my work.

LAND GRID:

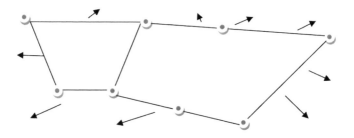

Adapt the placement of the copper to the property corners while keeping the spacing to approximately six feet apart. The grid will extend farther; however, this guarantees the integrity of the grid even if several of the copper bits are moved.

You can buy 1/8" copper pipe and cut it into stakes and pound it into the ground. I prefer to take an old screw driver and poke a hole in the ground, round it out, drop a penny and step on it to close. It's less likely someone will find it and remove it or trip over it. In time, copper stakes can work their way out and can snag pets or machinery, so, I normally just place them near fence posts or buildings and use the copper pieces in open areas.

I've had a few students that recycle copper wires from cords and cut them into one-inch segments. When laying a grid in a room, these are easier to tuck in along the floor boards or around the moldings. Take some painter's tape and tape pennies out of sight under furniture and behind pictures. If the resident knows why they are there, she will normally leave them in place, so it is important that she understands the process and as much as possible assists you with the initial layout.

After the grid is complete, remember to diffuse energy out into the local area in order to prevent negative energy from encircling the grid.

Manifesting With the Use of Vortex Energy

Stand near the Vortex and hold a seed thought affirming that it has come to pass. For example: "I now celebrate my financial freedom." "All good things surround me." "Radiant health flows through me." "I am whole, complete and perfect in all aspects of my life."

UNDERGROUND WATER FLOW

I was once invited to assist a group of Native Americans in doing energy work in a hospital. Apparently there were certain beds in one particular area of the hospital that were privately known as the "death beds." The nurses confided that they refused to use those beds because anyone assigned there invariably died.

Immediately, several of the investigative team began to fashion dowsing rods out of some of the local bushes. They cut off branches that formed a perfect "Y" and whittled away the foliage so a person could grasp two ends in his hands to point the long end of the stick in front as he walked over the area. Water witching, as it is also known, has been a centuries-old practice to find underground water, mineral and other buried items. It was fascinating to watch. The stick would point straight ahead, and then suddenly wrench downward. An assistant would mark the spot with tape, and they would continue to weave back and forth across the area, continuing the process outdoors using small flags to indicate wherever the dowsing rod had indicated a location.

It was determined from the dowsing that there was an underground water flow that needed to be redirected. Sizeable copper stakes were driven into the corner of the foundation and anchored around the sides of the building. Then three men took a 15 foot copper pipe and turned it parallel to the earth. They made a grand show of pushing energy away from each side of the building while the rest of us chanted and clapped, apparently to build the energy and call in favorable spirit help.

A local librarian confirmed that there was, indeed, a large water table under the property, later showing the team maps from a geological survey. As far as I know, moving the underground water flow did the trick.

Should you discover a problem related to underground water consider using the Copper Vortex Screen as explained earlier in this chapter. However, I was instructed that it is essential to drive the copper at least three feet underground. Again, I caution that stakes will eventually work their way up and can become hazardous. I am confident that should you need to redirect a water flow, you or a member of your team, will come up with a miraculous solution.

Creating a Copper Grid to move out Negative Energy

Using small bits of copper spaced less than six feet apart, start at the back corner of the room, form a U shape, and leave the door area open. Take copper in both hands and move from the far corner out, through the doorway, sweeping the energy in front of you as you walk. Finish by placing copper at the door to completely enclose the area in a grid. Continue this process room by room, returning to each room when done to visualize happy, prosperous, comforting energy, adding restful energy to the bedroom, and creative and good health energy to the entire building.

Grid to Secure Sacred Space

This process is achieved through active visualization. The more focused you are in your intention, the stronger your results will be. This technique can be used for a city, a property, a home, a business space, a building, a room, or a small area within a room.

Please Note: If you intend to screen a shared space, unless you are the owner, it is respectful to discuss your intentions with others sharing the space. You will find that doing this exercise as a group can be exceptionally powerful.

1. Find a comfortable position in which to stand in the center of the area you wish to screen.

2. Separate your feet and balance your weight between them.

3. Begin by visualizing 4 posts at the corners within the area to be screened. If it's an exceptionally large area you may choose to visualize pillars instead of posts. If you are screening a home, it would be the four corners of the house or the four corners of the property line. I recommend you do both separately as it serves to amplify the energy.

4. Now imagine that at the top of each post is a line that connects to the next post with a large floor length curtain hanging from it. Draw this drape full circle around all of the posts until it has totally encompassed the interior space. Seal it where it rejoins itself.

5. Picture a large awning covering the top of the posts creating a tent. Secure the edges so it becomes totally enclosed.

6. Extend the canopy under the tent and secure the lower edges.

7. Now visualize the floor slanting downwards to a drain at the center with a vacuum attached to the underside of the drain. Begin to suck all of the energy out of the

contained area. The more sensitive you are the more you will observe large dark spots and other garbage sliding into the drain.

8. When the area is clear a small metal ball will rattle in the drain trap. This marble is to prevent energy from seeping back up from the drain. Yet it leaves the drain open to continually clear all negative energy tracked into the environment.

9. Now open the windows and doors and mentally invite in all who you would prefer to join you in your sanctuary: friends, family, clients, helpful people, pets, etc.

10. You can use Holy Water to bless and seal the portals.

11. Open a sky light and invite in Divine healing energy and ask for a spiritual blessing to guard and uplift the area and all who enter. (see below: Consecration or Blessing of the Space or Home)

12. Dedicate the space to this new energy and with your clear intent require all energy that is not compatible with your intent to continue to be cleared through the drain.

13. Visualize several paths running out from your doors into the surrounding areas and continuing out into the world. See these paths opening a clear and inviting path for all whom you wish to invite into this space.

14. Mark the space with your blessing and affirm that it is so. (AMEN, HO)

CONSECRATION OR BLESSING OF THE SPACE OR HOME

Once the grid is in place, there is a clear energy field waiting to be charged with intention. I set the thought form energy and lay boundaries for the property or the home by verbally stating the owner's preferences. I normally ask the client what they want in the space; i.e.: play and social interaction, serenity and retreat, home and health, privacy and seclusion, etc. Then I pronounce it. Again, be sensitive to your client's religious preference. Here are a couple of examples:

"I now invite in Nature and all spirits who harmonize with creating a sacred sanctuary. Let all who pass these boundaries and enter this land be respectful and helpful to the land and the people who live here. Aho!" (Let it be so. Ho or Aho are indigenous terms equivalent to Amen.)

"Beloved Lord God, I beseech you to grant to this client a place of sanctuary, a place of wellness and retreat. May all that enter here within come in the spirit of respect. May those who live here be inspired and uplifted, seeking Your guidance and prospering in alignment with Your Divine will, in the name of Jesus Christ our Lord and Savior, Amen."

You get the gist of it. Basically, it's a consecration of the space and a setting of intention for how the energies will align. The basic, "Let there be peace, let there be wellness, let there be prosperity," serves just as well. Many times the clients choose to say their own prayers and place the blessing or have their minister come in later and do it in a private ceremony. Whatever works is what I recommend.

If the blessing will happen later, I just privately say a small invocation that the will of the client is respected and only that which is in alignment with her wishes can enter this sanctuary. Let's face it, it's better to put up a temporary screen than to have nothing in place and the first energies that imprint be of anger or frustration.

Releasing the Ghost

So how do I release a ghost?

Great question!

Much depends on how long the individual has been dead. The trick is, the ghost must be willing to connect with the spirit realm and be pulled across. Telling a ghost it is dead, is as if someone was telling you in an unknown foreign language that you were dead. The ghost just doesn't understand, as the subconscious mind, which is literally what the ghost is, does not have the ability to think and, therefore, cannot realize the full intent of what is being communicated. Remember, the key here is memory. If it responds to this statement, the ghost is most likely reacting to some old criticism that it recalls. It is important to keep in mind that the ghost is merely an animated collage of someone's memories and is not responding to you, but rather to its own history.

I once attended a séance where a couple of ghosts came forward and spoke. The host, offhandedly told these ghosts that they were dead. Both ghosts had different reactions. The first believed she was being threatened, and that "You're dead" meant that the host intended to kill her. The second ghost humored the host, pretending to play along. This ghost remembered a mentally imbalanced aunt and mistook the conversation as being with this relative, thus agreeing to the accusation before returning to its haunt. Neither ghost was released. Remember, ghosts are real people. Can you imagine the response you would get from telling a stranger on the street that he was dead?

I am always looking for new insights on how to clear ghosts. Because of my psychic abilities, I can see whether or not these techniques are effective. So far, the method I use seems to be the most reliable.

The longer the ghost has been dead, the easier it becomes to release it. I normally tell the ghost that someone is calling them. The ghost's response is usually to name someone they expect to see, and look around for that person. If the person named has passed over, he will immediately appear and will extend a hand and ask the ghost to step over. Most ghosts are highly receptive to accompanying their spiritual guide, and I can actually watch them move with their companion into the light. In other cases, a spirit guide may impersonate the person that has been named and assist the ghost in crossing. It is important to note that if the person that the ghost expects is someone they wish to avoid, this process will not work.

So, if the ghost is difficult and will not connect with someone on the other side, I often escort them through. I tell it that we must go somewhere and the ghost will normally respond by telling me somewhere it expects to go, like to a church, a reunion, a grocery store, etc. I agree with the ghost and accompany it. Once we arrive, I tell the ghost that someone, such as the minister, a family member or the grocer wishes to talk with them. Once again, that individual or a spirit "in drag" connects with the ghost and invites it over. There has only been once that this last reunion technique did not prove successful.

As you will most likely have a psychic on your paranormal team, you will be able to receive immediate confirmation that the ghost has cleared. The client and at least one team member will notice an energy shift. Don't fuss too much over the ghosties. A prayer that they be assisted from the other side often does the trick.

Myself, if I'm clearing the property on my own, I like to sit in a comfortable chair at home and do the work through astral travel. I visualize myself on the property, seek out the ghost and tell it I'd like to show it something pretty, then I just walk it into the light and the ghost follows me. Doing the work from the astral plane allows me to overview the location and see everything from a totally spiritual perspective. I'm able to pick up on anything I've overlooked.

Debriefing the Client

After I've finished with the Spiritual work, it's time for the homework. This basically involves telling the client what I experienced in clearing the location, and any recommendations that I feel necessary to bring the situation into balance.

If there are any physical reasons contributing to the phenomena, such as loose pipes, trees hitting the building, animals nesting in the house, a gas leak or loose wires, I make sure to write these things down and insist that they are repaired. Once, I discovered a wind chime was banging against a wall. When it was relocated, the sound of footsteps on the wooden floor ceased.

Many times, there are emotional, psychological or self-medication issues that contribute to the client's ability to see spiritual phenomena. As appropriate, I will often recommend education on psychic or spiritual development. There are times I suggest the client return to a religious practice or begin to meditate. In situations where there is a mental health issue, I recommend treatment and offer a list of therapists and doctors that are comfortable working with patients who are having spiritual encounters. In the case of drug or alcohol abuse, I offer referrals and straight talk. Addiction is a disease and if left untreated, it leads to death.

I often wonder how much I truly help others. As the ghosts are not in a situation where they are suffering, I believe it is only in my imagination that they appreciate being freed.

It's sad to say that most of our movies spook us up and give us so many horrific ideas about spiritual phenomena that often the truth is totally lost. If the average person could come to more general knowledge about ghosts, I feel people would be less traumatized by the encounter and more capable of clearing the phenomena for themselves. I must admit there are some films where the writer and producers have touched into the truth, but these are often staged with such intensely frightening story lines that the viewer comes away fearful of any such encounter. But that's film making.

The conscious mind understands this, but, of course, the subconscious mind has no ability to discriminate and accepts everything as fact. It sees what it sees, and without the logic filter of the reasoning mind, the subconscious responds accordingly. That's why horror movies are so frightening. The problem is the subconscious will remember the movie as if it was real and respond with the same measure of terror to natural spiritual phenomena. Getting beyond this preconditioning has been a struggle for me. Embarrassing to admit, there was a paranormal investigation where I, in broad daylight, even though I was surrounded by several companions, screamed. For a fraction of a second I remembered a gory segment of a movie and overlaid it with the situation. Pure terror overwhelmed my reason. There was no way I could undo my reaction. Needless to say, my client was even more distraught when I left. Oops! She sold her house and moved shortly afterwards.

"Do not fear what you do not understand, for with understanding comes acceptance." Often, I reflect on these words from Walter Rhineder. I think somehow, the most I can ever do is to offer my clients some understanding and lend a hand to help them find their balance. For me, it's an extraordinary life. I have such fabulous adventures, I'm never quite sure what will unfold as I turn up the music to *Ghostbusters* and head out to once again investigate another haunting.

Ouija Board

I hear, so often, people who have discovered a ghost through a session with the Ouija Board. They will call, wanting me to, not only, release the ghost, but also take their fears away.

First and foremost, the Ouija Board is a tool. Just like a knife or a chainsaw, your concern need not be for the tool, rather for the operator.

When a person uses an Ouija Board, he will draw in whatever he is asking for. Imagine a group at a party. They are drinking and showing off, and someone has a great idea to pull out the Ouija Board to summon, who knows what. Great! Let's not forget that like will attract like. A spirit who enjoys a good party, who may also be in a similarly altered state, will be happy to come through and sensationalize the moment. Hey! It's a party; everyone's blitzed, including the spirit. Now is the time for some scandalous entertainment. The party-goers got what they asked for, and now they blame the Ouija Board.

I recommend, if someone chooses to use an Ouija Board, he does so with a clear intent. He should ask specifically what he wants of the board and those present before he begins. It's good to remember, as above, so below. Just like certain individuals aren't attracted to certain gatherings in society, spirits have preferences too. A mischievous spirit won't be attracted to a group that doesn't want to play horror games.

Also, when using an Ouija Board—just like in using a radio—if you don't like what you're hearing, turn the dial to another frequency. Having a specific intent is like having a specific radio channel—it gives the listener an idea of what he may expect to hear.

BASIC FENG SHUI FOR CLEARING & BALANCING ENERGIES

There are many ways to clear unwanted energies, including the use of smudging, Holy Water, prayers, music, chanting, color, and even clapping. The following procedures are used for clearing a property as well as the auric space around an individual.

The auric field, commonly known as the aura, is around every living thing including plants, water and rocks. It is created by the Chi or Life Force Energy of the individual. For those who can see auras, it appears like a shimmering light, much like heat rising off pavement. It seems to literally radiate off each individual, encapsulating them in a bubble of colored energy. This corona is often referred to as the halo, and can be seen in many paintings by famous artists.

In addition, the aura may have symbols of faith and often blessings or seals. These, combined with loving protection prayers, hang as translucent colors around the person. Sometimes negative thoughts or other harsh energies become trapped in the field, appearing as slashes of discordant color or images. Cleansing the Auric field is as simple and straightforward as cleaning the body or the building. What is important is to be thorough and to make a routine of it so as to keep the energies in balance.

Smudging - One of the most popular methods of dissipating negative influence around a person or environment is called smudging or saging. Sacred herbs or ritually prepared incense such as sage, sweet grass, Kinnikinnik, a specially blended tobacco, cedar, or copal are burned and the smoke is used to purify. All of these herbs are gathered and prepared for ceremonial and healing work in a sacred way. As the blessed herb burns, smoke is fanned through the aura or spread throughout the building into every space. Special attention is given to areas that have a dark or heavy vibration. It is fascinating to watch when the smoke refuses to be drawn into an area. It will roll back on itself or go around the blockage, often creating a silhouette of whatever is resisting the cleansing. The use of a fan or feather is particularly helpful, at this point. I normally slice the feather through the air and insert the burning bowl of herbs directly into the center of the blockage. This most always does the trick.

Holy Water - Holy Water, or water that has been blessed with spoken word or prayer, takes on different vibrations. Traditionally, the blessing was done by a priest, rabbi, minister or holy person, often for a baptism or House Blessing. However, anyone with clear intention can turn water into Holy Water through the use of prayer or spoken word. Water from sacred sites can also be used. Sprinkling blessed water upon the earth is the best way to cleanse violently spilled blood.

The scientific work done by Masaru Emoto of Japan illustrates that these blessings actually do affect the water. Dr. Emoto placed sterile water in a glass container and then wrote a single uplifting word on the jar. The resulting crystalline water pattern was astonishingly beautiful as well as proving consistent in repeated experiments.

I use Holy Water in all my House Blessings to anoint the thresholds of every door. This blessing keeps both physical and spiritual intruders away and prevents Earth Spirits from entering the woodwork of the home.

Many Earth Spirits are like the spiritual equivalent of a ladybug. They normally live in the wood of a tree or, when unavailable, may inhabit the wood within a home, appearing in door panels and other grained wood. They do their own thing, not bothering anyone or causing any harm. Yet, to many people, a bug is a bug regardless of whether it's a lady or not. They want it out. So, placing a little Holy Water on the door lintel guarantees Earth Spirits will evacuate the premises. Personally I like having Earth Spirits on my property.

Living Energy - Life! Anything that is alive reminds us, subtly, that things change and life continues. It is good for the psyche as well as the soul. Plants, water, animals and stones all have Auric fields—they generate movement and a continued supply of new energy.

Green growing vegetation, not only, has an ability to cleanse the air, it also heals the soul. It is important that the plants have enough water and light. I recommend easy maintenance plants such as cactus and African Violets. It is always a delight when they bloom adding a spray of flowers to the room. If light is scarce, spending $5.00 a week on small bouquet is as effective as a plant. Flowers are a great solution, for any individual who lacks a green thumb.

Another great way to refresh the energy is to have a small fountain or even a fish tank. Water is a great conductor of energy and if the water is blessed it will filter negativity influences and constantly distribute the blessing into the air. Many health care facilities, where people are in crisis, have fountains or aquariums in their lobbies for the therapeutic effect. I often wonder if they realize the spiritual effect as well.

Pets are not only affectionate, they're a great distraction. They help us forget our concerns and focus in the here and now. They can also alert us to danger, so we feel more settled when they are calm. Stroking an animal has been documented to lower blood pressure and helps trigger endorphins, small chemicals in the brain, which are essential for positive feelings.

Pet rocks are also a living force that brings energy into the environment. Whether it is a garden variety rock or a special gem stone, the "Rock People" as they are referred to in Native American circles, have a wonderful effect that either grounds or uplifts the handler. Rocks that are dense, heavy and opaque (light doesn't pass through these little puppies) have a truly stabilizing effect. Stones that uplift energy are light in density, faceted, clear or somewhat translucent. Light normally forms into prisms as it passes through these sparkly gems.

Light - Light is essential and, whereas I perceive it as a living vibration, I am not clear how it has been scientifically categorized. Depression often occurs in individuals who live in lowlight environments. Sunlight is often an important part of the prescription for those who suffer from Light Deprivation Syndrome, a condition where the body lacks the vitamins that come from natural light. Adding a multi-spectrum light would also allow plants to be grown in a darker area. Or better yet, I recommend a small tubular hole through the ceiling. These mini-skylights are inexpensive to install but can really add optimal light to a dingy area. Using mirrors to reflect light, the vegetation and the sky from outdoors also strengthens the positive energy.

Color - Color has its own unique vibration and stimulates an emotional response from people. Hues of red and pink normally arouse passion. Blues and greens are restful and soothing. Yellows and oranges are uplifting and stimulating. So, depending on what the area is used for, splash in a bit of appropriate color. Painting is the easiest way to shift energy with color. Adding art, happy photos, fabric, pillows or rugs can dramatically shift the energy, as well as be more calming, or, if preferred, stimulating for the occupant.

Scent - Each person is influenced differently by smell, yet nature's smells, such as woodlands and flowers, are soothing to most. Smells of spices and home cooking can be comforting. Lighting candles, burning incense or spritzing air freshener are often effective in shifting the energies.

Children and animals relax and sleep deeper when the smells associated with the parent are in their bedding. So, I recommend wearing an old shirt for a day or two, and then placing it in the bed near the child or pet. This works extremely well if traveling with a pet. The smell gives comfort, and they are less likely to fuss.

Sound - Prayers, singing, chanting, laughter, chimes, music, and even clapping can shift the energy of a location. All sound is vibration, and the more joyful the sound, the more uplifted the energy that is released. In dark basements, besides adding light, I often have the owner place bells and wind chimes to tap each time they pass. This adds pleasant sounds into the dim space.

In Peru, Shamans will actually clap and stomp around, in order to drive out lower influences and welcome in beneficial spirits. I once participated in a cleansing ceremony where participants, after being sprayed with cheap perfume, had to go to the wall and shake, stomp, and pull off their negativity. The rest of those gathered in the circle, clapped and whistled to assist in driving away the malevolent forces. It was a primal experience, but exceptionally freeing. As a rite of passage, it was an effective aide in reinforcing the belief that old, unwanted personal garbage had truly been discarded.

Movement - Shuffling cards, rocking, dancing, and hanging objects that flutter, jingle or twirl are fabulous for keeping energy charged in a positive way. Movement is also extremely playful, and can bring a sense of youthful pleasure. I often suggest placing a hanging mobile of laminated family photos over the baby's crib or setting an animated music box in the children's room.

Mirrors - Placing mirrors in a room can create a more open and spacious look because they reflect light. Be aware that placing two mirrors back to back is not the best idea, as they can amplify a vortex or even create a new one. Always check to see where the bathroom mirrors are located, and make sure that there is not another silver-backed mirror on the opposite side of the same wall. Normally newer mirrors are not painted with silver, so there is rarely a problem.

XI. Report and Follow-Up

It's important to document your research. If you don't, there will be so much information forgotten. Should you need to recall the events, you will find, over time, that you'll struggle to determine what location and what phenomena was experienced. Write it down and pull it together in a report.

If you have done the Initial Interview, as I suggested, you can actually enter information into your computer or electronic note pad as you do the interview. You can also have one of your team members fill out the form and forward it to you.

Now take your notes and record what you and your team experienced. Document your conclusion and the resolve you intend to take. Forward this to your team members for editing. Now, you have a report to share with your client, and refer to, as you desire.

I will print out a paper copy and put it in a binder so I can refer back to several reports side by side.

Please, if you plan to share information with anyone other than the client or your team, label them and remove all personal information. I like to name them by the primary experience, *The Case of the Water Spirit*, *The Ghost who came for Dinner*, *The Mt Rainier Apparition*, etc. I will often leave confidential information off my team's copy of the report, especially if I don't know the member very well.

I once had a team member who invited her psychic friend to come along. It's hard to say, "No," when they just show up. This did not go well, as this "friend" took it on herself to call the client and give unsolicited information. The client had the courtesy to call me and ask, "What's up with this?" I was able to defuse a problem before it turned into a crisis. Remember, know your team and be clear what is okay and not okay. Yes, I have investigations that I allow friends, family and new members to assist, but these are situations where I have confidence that no one can create a horror show. I'll leave the investigation to my team and escort the spectators through in order for them to have a positive experience.

Ego is such a major issue with doing this type of work. People want to feel adequate and part of the solution. However, if they don't think it through, the consequences can be unnecessarily disruptive. You need a strong ego in order to do this work, but you need to befriend it and help it to understand that the more professional you can be, the better the overall result for everyone.

I make it a habit to give all team members a chore, such as laying a grid, screening the vortex, or clearing the ghost-ies, so that they, not only, can learn through the experience, but also feel that they actively contributed to the solution. Having active participants keeps the entire situation much more manageable.

SAMPLE OF FINAL REPORT

www.teresacarol.com

PARANORMAL INVESTIGATION REPORT
The Case of the Unbalanced Family

Initial Interview: January 25, 20XX: 2:00PM

Location: Starbucks (address), WA 253 (Phone #)

Participants: Teresa Carol, the names of my participating team members, the names of the unbalanced family members.

Investigation Date: January 29, 20XX: 10:00AM

Investigative Assistants: Teresa Carol, the names of my participating team members

Contact: client and spouse

Phone: 253-XXX-XXX Text

E-Mail: Client's.email@email.com

Location: premise street address and description such as 50 year old house, 20acres near river, formerly part of a family estate owned by client's grandfather, etc.

Family Members/Ages: List the names of the family members which I have omitted for privacy. Client, Spouse, female child 16, female child 14, male child 11

Family Support: Client's Mom = name, Sister in Law = name.

Religion: Spiritual; fan of the Pennsylvania Psychic

Ethnic Background: Caucasian

Pets: (list names and species),dog, cats, turtle, snakes and chickens

Background: The husband and wife were estranged for several years as spouse went to prison for drug use. He currently appears to be in recovery and committed to his family. Client seems to be highly empathic and has been in the hospital 3 times over the last 6 months. She has grown reclusive and suffers from a number of physical and emotional problems.

Client Reports: The family experience "seeing apparitions", missing items, hearing voices. The residents have experienced the feeling of someone there and also a feeling of someone watching. They have seen unusual shadows and mild poltergeist activity. The attic area appears grey and they have had occurrences in the loft of the barn in which the spouse reports he felt as if he was being chased out. Since they moved to the property they feel as if they have had a constant run of "bad luck." The client had no prior health problems and believes something at the property is making her ill.

The property was part of a dairy farm for over 100 years. The last tenant raised animals for slaughter and apparently allowed the animals to starve because of lack of income. Spouse and Client report they have found a pig carcass on the area where they intend to grow crops.

The client hopes to stay in the home and crop farm the land. They are currently raising eggs and poultry for income.

Purpose of Investigation: Client desires to live in peace, and client wants to regain her balance. Client is quite adamant that she wants her life back.

The first part of this report is basically your Initial Interview. I often type this up, omitting last names and contact information, and provide it to my team member and the client when we arrive for the investigation. Some of my team like me to email it to them, and they add their own information to it for their files.

FINDINGS

Back Entry: On the left side of the home, near the back door, the power panel is showing an excessive reading of electrical energy.

On entering the home, there is a nervous, tingly energy. It is happy and hopeful, but intense.

Kitchen: The energy in the kitchen is blurred as if looking through a distorted piece of glass. There are several areas of energy that have a sharp, spiky feeling, like bugs crawling. One team member noticed an active area on the left of the stove. She felt as if someone was cooking.

Dining Room: The dining room is the heart of the house. The energy here is warm and uplifting. This appears to be a gathering spot for the family; the area feels spacious, open and inviting. One team member came in contact with a past resident. Her name is Sara, and she says, "My home." Sara seems to be watching over the house and the family. She doesn't want to scare anyone. She moves between the kitchen, dining room and living room fireplace. Sara is a Ghost.

Master Bedroom: There is a strong physical smell, it could be marijuana or it could be the septic tank. I feel a severe lower backache pain. The mirror seems to have shadows and when using the compass near it, the dial swings from 100° to 55°. A large vortex dominates from the center of the bed, through the walls and outside to the corner of the home.

Girl's Room: My right eye hurts and someone suggests that if I place a marble in the eye it will not hurt as much and should keep my face from distorting. Over the pillow of the client's daughter, the compass continually rotates 180°

Boy's Room: There is a strong smell of earth, could be septic. It is intensely cold. I have an aching feeling at the back of my head and feel stir crazy as if being confined.

Hallway: There is a 6-foot length where the energy is amplified; I feel a sense of depression and despair there. Along the hallway on both sides of the wall the energy registers extremely high. Using the compass there is a deviation of 25° to 180° in a short area. This definitely indicates a magnetic disturbance. There are strong EMF readings along the hallway in this area especially entering the master bedroom.

Living Room: The furniture in this room is lined up along the walls as if it is a waiting room. There is a definite need for Feng Shui or other energy cures to make the space more inviting.

Garage: There is a strong distortion of energy. It is difficult to remain upright. I feel excessively called to go up the ladder and hide. There is a sharp warning, "Do not come up! Back off!" I see a man named Jeremiah being stabbed in the back as he attempts to flee up the ladder.

Barn: The barn with the chickens feels as if there needs to be some music or some energy to create playfulness; more lighthearted energy. Music would sooth the birds. Right now, there is a strong feeling of being in survival mode; a desperation to achieve.

Property: At the far east of the property is a creek running along the base of a ridge. I notice thick fog or vapor that seems to constantly collect and dissipate. In 1889 Samuel Miles, a scout for the Northwest Territories, passed from Colorado to California. On his way up to Canada, he was ambushed by frontier men for his horse, his pack animal, and his gun. His corpse was left under the trees near the bushes by the Creek.

This site was a camping area for a nomadic group of Native Americans who wandered to the ocean for salt and fish. They foraged, gathered and hunted from the Everett area down as far as Portland. In the spring or late fall of 1842, several criminals, who had been run out of California, passed through the area. Because of their prior experience with savage Indians, the outlaws ambushed and killed the group of peaceful Native Americans. Eight individuals were killed, including two outlaws, three women and two children.

A team member came across a woman, named Sara, who lived on the land in another home. Sara seems to hang out near the kitchen and walk to the fireplace area where she had a garden. None of the original structures are currently standing. The house may have been west of the current residence and the barn approximately where the garage is today.

Sara and her husband Jeremiah may have been the first homesteaders. Sara and Jeremiah Berns were killed in an attack by three marauders. Jeremiah was away from the house when Sara, three children and a second woman ran to hide in the barn. Sara defended them from her location in the loft until she ran out of ammunition and was shot. Jeremiah returned to the burning house and ran to look for his family. He was stabbed in the back as he was climbing the ladder. The other woman was taken by the men. The neighbors noticed the house on fire and came to investigate and were able to run off the outlaws. They took in the children and sold the land to pay for the children's upkeep.

There are power lines that parallel the highway in front of the house that may put off a certain level of EMF and emit radon radiation. This can add to the excess EMF readings we observed in the house.

DETERMINATION & RECOMMENDATIONS

SEPTIC SYSTEM: This is a high priority! There is odor and signs of a septic problem. The owner needs to be notified and the problem resolved for health safety. I would strongly recommend checking with the Tenant/Landlord authorities as to the best way to guarantee a quick and complete cleanup of this health hazard.

Electro Magnetic Frequency (EMFS): The electrical system of the home is antiquated and needs to be brought up to code. The power panel box and inside wiring gives off excessive energy readings. There appears to be the original knob and tube wiring in the attic and walls which may greatly add to the EMF readings. In addition, there is also a power line running directly in front of the house which can contribute to these readings. I would recommend the Clients speak to the power company about acceptable limits of electrical discharge in the home environment. If the levels are documented outside of the norm the landlord should be made aware of a potential fire liability.

I strongly recommend all fire alarms are in place and monitored monthly. Also, the family needs to have an emergency evacuation plan in place.

ENITY ATTACHMENT: Because of Client's empathic nature she has drawn in two Viet Nam soldiers. Nat and his buddy Vicente have been attached to the Client since the 1960's. These two young men were emotionally bonded and have attempted to be born into the family as twins. The team has transitioned them successfully into the light and they are now free to continue their journey. These individuals were not harmful; rather disorientated and sometimes overly medicated. I have removed the entities and explained basic spiritual clearing to the Client and the family member who were present. I do have a concern that either the Client or one of the entities is suffering from a mental health imbalance. I strongly recommend that the Client consistently cleanse her energy field and if she continues to have difficulties, there may be a medical concern, for which she may need to seek professional help.

GHOSTS: All Ghosts have been successfully cleared from the premises.

Frontier settlers: Sara and Jeremiah Bern, Bearns or Burns, were murdered by a group of wandering outlaws. Sara was shot in the right side of her lower back and bled out; Jeremiah was stabbed in the back between his shoulder blades. One Team member has cleared Sara, and I have cleared Jeremiah. No future action required.

Samuel A. Miles: Canadian Scout for the Northwest Territories was robbed and killed near the creek.

Indian Spirits: Several Indian spirits, one male, two females, and children, still roam the creek causing the appearance of a mist. They were massacred by outlaws.

Small male child: Paul or Peter?—A team member will release.

Fox: Hit by car around 1961.

FAMILIAR - EARTH SPIRIT HELPER: Client's young daughter was a Wiccan in past life and has retained the ability to work with the Earth and the Earth Spirits. A familiar or earth spirit has been attracted to her and sleeps on the pillow near her head. This is a positive spirit and I recommend she learns to communicate with it and uses its ability to assist in healing the land.

VORTEX: A naturally occurring vortex is situated between the driveway and the center of the Master Bedroom. I recommend that Client does not sleep in the vortex. I will screen the vortex so that it vents between the house and the driveway.

Vortex - From Wikipedia, the free encyclopedia

A vortex (plural: vortices) is a spinning, often turbulent, flow of fluid or air. Any spiral motion with closed streamlines is vortex flow. The motion of the fluid swirling rapidly around a center is called a vortex. The speed and rate of rotation of the fluid in a free (irrotational) vortex are greatest at the center, and decrease progressively with distance from the center, whereas the speed of a forced (rotational) vortex is zero at the center and increases proportional to the distance from the center. Both types of vortices exhibit a pressure minimum at the center, though the pressure minimum in a free vortex is much lower.

Manifesting With Vortex Energy - Stand near the Vortex and hold a seed thought affirming that it has come to pass. Example:"I now celebrate my financial freedom." "All good things surround me." "Radiant health flows through me." "I am whole, complete and perfect in all aspects of my life."

ACTION TO RESOLVE

Septic: Client responsibility - Please immediately research tenant/landlord laws and request the problem is attended to in a timely manner.

High Electrical Readings: Client responsibility - Please consult with the power company informing them of the knob and tube wiring in the house and the results of the EMF meters. Please keep all Fire Detectors in working condition!

Entity Attachments: Action Complete—Both entities have been cleared and Client's auric field strengthened. I strongly recommend that the Client and the family receive credible psychic and spiritual awakening training to avoid further empathic attachments.

Ghosts: Action Complete—All Ghosts have been released and sent to the light. No further action is required.

Familiar: Client responsibility—I recommend the young daughter learns about the practice of Wicca. It is further recommended that she learns to communicate with the earth spirit and uses its ability to heal the land.

Mental Health Imbalance: Action Complete/Client responsibility—It is my hope that clearing the entities will remove much of the mental imbalance. However, if the client continues to have difficulty I would recommend medical examination of hormones. The smoking of marijuana and drinking of excessive alcohol can also cause a mentally overwhelmed state; therefore I recommend the client use discernment with these substances.

Vortex: I have screened the vortex so that it vents between the house and the driveway.

Land Clearing and Blessing: Several of the team will perform a water and property blessing to draw in health, vitality and to balance the land with nature.

Resetting Positive Energies:

1. Please relocate Dining Room mirror so that it is not facing the front door. Be careful not to place any mirrors back to back.

2. Please spiritually clear the mirror in the Master Bedroom as it is reflecting the vortex.

3. The house should be coined (a copper grid set in place) to straighten the energies and spiritually protect the premises and occupants. The three kids have participated in placing the coins externally on the four corners of the house and the team has preformed the blessing. Action Completed.

4. The family needs to understand energy flows and begin to create an environment that is open for playful interaction and comfort. I would suggest studying Feng Shui. Several suggestions were made for the rearrangement of the front room as it is important that it not remain a waiting room. Settle in and enjoy the property; the energy is basically good and the members of the family are Earth Stewards.

Note to Client: As we discussed, I would advise that you pay a Home Inspector before purchasing this home. The property is good and you can have wonderful success if you are motivated. The house, however, may need to be totally replaced. I would recommend you consider a Double Wide Mobile Home or new construction if you decide to buy this specific property. You might be able to exclude the house and purchase only the farm. Stay alert. You may find that another nearby property with a quality older home comes up for sale in the next two years. Be educated and you will make a wiser decision.

Completed by Teresa Carol 4.26.2013

| The Case of the Unbalanced Family - Client Last Name - County www.teresacarol.com (253) XXX-XXXX 4/12/13 | 1 |

Photos: I like to include a few photos in the report; this really helps everyone's memory. If you take a team picture and label the member's first names, it's a lot easier for the client to identify who told her what. I don't recommend you put anyone's last name on the public documents because you never know who might end up with them.

I am always being asked by the home owner, "What did that team member mean when he said…?" Normally the client will give you a physical description of the individual and then she proceeds to tell you something that you absolutely have no idea what she is talking about. It's so much easier to have the client look at the team photo and decide who she spoke with. And if everyone was wearing their badge, the client might even recall the team member's name.

Candid shots of the client and family in the background can help the team remember a specific investigation, especially after your team has done two or three similar cases.

I like to take a photo of the property and the hotspots. It's interesting to see if anything shows up. Even though there was no one in the house at the time the pictures were taken, in *The Case of the Ghost Children*, you could see the faces of children looking out of the front windows. Also, in the photo of the home in *The Case of the Unseen Playmates*, a large fir tree on the front lawn appears to have a bubble of white light around it. These are great additions to your report and help to document the activity.

Back it Up: Make sure you back up all your files and photos. The good news is that I always print a hard copy of my investigations, but the bad news is that I've lost much of my information because of technical problems with my computers. Ah, and there was the case where I had set my camera down on the stove to write something on my clip-board. When I turned around, I found that "the ghost" had taken it. I had to believe the homeowner as I was alone in the kitchen, or at least I thought I was. Hmm?

XII. Glossary

Ascension: To rise upward or attain Christ Consciousness. A term used when an individual matures beyond the physical plane and physically rises into the spiritual realms.

Affirmation: To state as fact. A declaration of what is. A word or mantra used to recondition the mind in order to create a preferred reality.

Akashic Records: Akasha is from the Sanskrit meaning "Primary Substance". The imperishable record of life; often referred to as the Universal Mind, the Collective Conscious; God's memory. On this vibrational plane all thoughts, words and actions are recorded. This is not for judgment, rather an accurate memory recording. This Crystalline record contains the knowledge of all time, including each individual's personal information. This information is believed to be stored in the Akashic Library, which is perceived to be written on the filaments of time much in the same way human memory is stored within the brain.

Angel: An immortal servant of God. In the Physical Realm they resemble humans with wings and are known to be loving, helpful beings. In other realms they appear less human and more bird like.

Animal Spirit: The spirit of a deceased animal, such as family pets or even the ghost of an animal. It is important that it not be confused with a Spirit Animal, which is a spirit using an animal form to symbolically communicate its strengths. See Spirit Animal

Ankh: An ancient Egyptian symbol shaped like at T with an oval on top. The circle represents the spiritual, the horizontal line represents the mental, the vertical line represents matter descending into the psychical and the flow of the line around the ankh denotes the emotional.

Apparition: A popular name for ghost or spirit. A term used for any spiritual phenomena that does not appear to be of this physical world. These images may be one from any number of different types of Spirits, consisting of individuals who have died, individuals who are Nature or Earth Spirits, or other inter-dimensional beings. These images can also be energies, such as thought forms, vortexes, Ley Lines or emotional energies or even a true ghost: a Subconscious Mind which has become fractured from its Higher Conscious and Conscious companions.

Apport: An object passed through from the Astral Realms most often at a séance. This object may have been teleported from another location on the Earth or another physical realm. Some objects that have been reported as falling from the air during a séance include coins, pebbles, gems, flowers, and even small birds, fish and frogs.

Astral Realms: The total expanse of all reality beyond the physical including the stars and the space between them.

In this realm, spirit is unlimited by space or time. All exists simultaneously in a web of interconnectedness.

Astral Travel: The act of separating the spiritual body from the physical and connecting it into the Astral Realms. This out-of-body experience happens with all individuals when they go to sleep. It is through Astral Travel that the Higher Conscious is able to remain connected with the Spiritual Realms.

Auric Field/Aura: An electro-magnetic energy field surrounding and emanating from all living forms including plants, water and rocks. It is created by the Chi or Life Force Energy of the life form. It appears to literally radiate off each individual encapsulating them in a bubble of colored energy. The aura may also contain symbols or marks.

Automatic Writing: Writing that is either influenced or controlled by an outside intelligence while the writer is in an altered state of consciousness. This form of spiritual communication is often used for the purpose of gathering information or guidance.

Clipboard: A thin, portable board on to which paper is clipped for writing. In paranormal investigation, an essential tool for clutching when startled.

Chakra: An energy center within the physical body, which receives and transmits energy. It is thought to be spinning wheels, which create vortexes within the body.

Channel: A psychic or medium who allows information to flow through his consciousness in order to give guidance and inspiration to others. It is possible all psychic insight is a form of channeling.

Channeling: The process of moving something through a conduit without damaging or affecting the object through which it passes for a predetermined purpose. Water is channeled through pipes, electricity is channeled through wires and consciousness can be channeled through a receptive Medium, known as a Channel.

Chi Energy: Life force, the energy that gives life to all living beings. The energy flow that is necessary for the physical form to become animate. It is sometimes referred to as ectoplasm.

Christ Consciousness: The highest level of spiritual consciousness attainable while in the physical body. It is the total and harmonious balance of the trinity within the individual. This awareness is the realization of higher consciousness that Jesus attained.

Clair-audience: Literally clear hearing or the ability to hear beyond the physical limits of sound. Often voices or messages received directly in the brain with no apparent outside origination.

Clair-cognizance: The clear knowing of previously unknown information that is received from an undetermined source. The individual appears plugged-in to this knowledge with complete understanding, including the ability to explain or apply the information. However, in most cases, this connection is quickly lost when no longer required.

Clair-voyance: Clear seeing that allows the individual to see into the spiritual realms and perceive spirits such as ghosts and other Apparitions or even shadows of past buildings and activities.

Clair-sentience: A form of sensitivity which allows the individual to perceive movement and other activities that cannot be perceived by the physical eye.

Conscious Mind: Also known as the Reasoning and Logical Mind. This is one of the three major aspects of the human consciousness that processes rational thought. As so, referred to as the thinking mind, which is able to draw a conclusion or resolve a problem; the intellect.

Cursed: To subject someone or something to negative thoughts or words. Some actually believe that these actions can disrupt the life of the recipient. Often used to explain when someone is experiencing a series of extreme negative situations or bad luck.

Dead: Anyone or anything that previously was functioning but no longer operates in the Physical Realm. A state of existence often observed in employees and in computers.

Debunk: To ridicule in an attempt to expose as false. Some skeptics attempt to discount others by the use of debunking.

Demons: Large, dark, vicious, dog-like beings from another dimension; often labeled as devils. If you find them in this reality someone had to have brought them in. I would be more concerned over the individual who would have brought them to the Physical Realm. They will attempt to return to their dimension and will only be aggressive if confronted. Seek professional help in releasing all Demons.

Devils: A title for an evil or destructive individual, one who defies the Will of God. The angel, Lucifer, was the first so labeled. A devil may be of any sex or any species.

Dingy: Drab, colorless, lacking the vibration of life energy.

Divining Rod and Dowsing Rod: A forked stick often carved from a Willow branch, which can be used as a tool to locate water or other objects buried beneath the earth. The user loosely holds the handles of the tool in each hand, pointing the third fork straight forward as he walks over a given area. The suspended portion will turn down toward the earth when the object is underfoot. This ancient form of divination, known as well-witching, has been a popular method to determine the best location to drill for water.

Divas: A title for a sensual or seductive female of any species.

Doohickey: Gismo, thingamajig, or more the more common term of thingamabob, is whatever physical object you think you need in that instant to get the job done. It is important to note, that as the moment shifts, so does the particular doohickey required.

Dowsing: A method of locating a person or object through the movement of objects such as a pendulum or divining rods which respond to sudden variations in energy.

Earth or Nature Spirits: Spirits that are a living, conscious characteristic of the planet. They are also known as the elementals; Earth, Air, Fire, Water, Metal and Wood. They have been referred to as tree spirits, spirits of the wind, water sprites, earth energies and such. One famous Earth Spirit or Elemental is the volcanic spirit known as the Goddess Pele of Hawaii.

Echovox Android App (Spirit-Box Radio): The Echovox is a radio that captures acoustic resonance that spirit presumably uses for communication.

Ectoplasm: More commonly known as Earth or Chi Energy. Ectoplasm is an old name for the energy substance that sustains the physical form. It can often appear as a vapor or gel and has been reported to leave a slick, gooey residue.

Ego Mind: Also known as the Memory or the Subconscious Mind. This part of the mind records information and experiences. Should at death, this part of the mind fracture from the Conscious and Higher Conscious Minds, it creates the phenomenon known as a ghost.

Elementals: See Earth Spirits.

Electromagnetic energy: The magnetic energy created from electric charges in motion. This energy can be recorded and creates a dramatic response when registered on the physical body.

EMF Meter: Electromagnetic Frequency Meter measures electromagnetic emissions from anything that creates energy. Emissions can be given off by such things as appliances, animal, power lines, etc. However, most EMF meters are designed to ignore these readings and focus on the erratic and fluctuating patterns that are associated with paranormal activity.

Emotional energy: A highly charged energy created by strong emotional feelings such as joy, fear, grief, longing or lust.

Empathic: The ability to absorb into oneself the emotions and feelings of another. Often the individual will be unable to determine which feelings are their own and which are felt by the other.

Energy: A substance of constant active matter or essence from which all is formed; vibration.

Energy Field: An area or space composed of intense, measurable energy, often having no apparent source.

ESP: Extra Sensory Perception: the awareness of something from a source other than the five physical senses.

Esoteric: Intended for a small group. Those things or ideas not publicly disclosed or understood. Often they are of a spiritual or unseen nature.

Ethereal: Highly defined. Heavenly

Evil: That which is discordant with Divine Will; that which causes good things to blend together in a disruptive way.

EVP: Electronic Voice Phenomena are electronically captured sounds that seem to resemble speech but are reportedly not the result of intentional recording. EVP are commonly found in recordings with static, stray radio transmissions, and background noise. Usually, EVP sounds are short, only a word or two.

Expansive Group Consciousness: Also known as the Universal Mind or Higher Conscious Mind; the level of consciousness that is intuitive and gathers awareness directly from the Spiritual Realm.

Extra-Sensory Perception (ESP): To gain awareness beyond the use of the ordinary five senses. The psychic gift often called clairsentience or clairvoyance.

Faeries, Fairies: Small, human like, winged beings from another dimension that often fly through vortexes into our reality and become trapped. They have an extraordinary ability to heal that appears magical in the Physical Realm.

Feng Shui: An ancient art of alignment which allows the harmonious and uplifting flow of energy creating a safe, beneficial environment. Feng Shui can be used as a cure for disruptive energy and can assist in removing unwanted spiritual phenomena.

Gateway: Another slang term used for vortex or portal or any of a number of openings between dimensions or realms.

Get-away: The physical act of making a hasty retreat from a less than favorable location. Often employed when there is concern for physical or psychological safety.

Ghost: A slang term for any apparition. A true ghost is the phenomena created by the disconnected Subconscious Mind of an individual who has died and continues to rerun its former life.

Giant: A large human individual that once migrated through a vortex in the Scandinavian regions of Europe. Trolls and dragons also passed through this same vortex.

Gismo: A thingamajig, doohickey or more the more common term of thingamabob, is whatever physical object you think you need in that instant to get the job done.Itis important to note, that as the moment shifts, so does the particular doohickey required.

Gnome: Small human-like people who prefer to live in old-growth forest areas and are the Guardians of the Trees.

Grand Adventure: The opportunity to have fun, figure something paranormal out, and make a few shekels to rub together.

Group Consciousness: The energy or tangible intention made manifest of the overall psychological climate of the group. The core or seed thought of the gathering which creates a separate life form which inter-dimensionally connects all group members and begins to manifest their intent into physical form.

Haunted: A term that refers to the location, object or person that continually receives visitation from an Apparition; traditionally the location where a ghost is frequently sighted.

Hermetic Philosophy: The teachings of Hermes Trismegistus who determined the seven basic Universal Laws. It has been noted that Jesus studied this philosophy in Egypt and based much of his works on the Hermetic Principles.

Higher Conscious Mind: The level of consciousness also known as the Universal Mind or Expansive Group Consciousness that is intuitive and gathers awareness directly from the Spiritual Realm.

Higher Self: The super-conscious mind, the Christ Conscious or expanded awareness of an individual. The I AM Self of an individual, the God awareness in a person.

Hints: Innuendos or unspoken warnings that something is not allowed without resulting in unfavorable consequences.

Hoax: A prank or lie constructed to deceive, often done for the attention or to discredit an authority.

Holy Water: Water that has been blessed or charged with positive energy in order to assist with wellness and the elimination of disruptive influences.

Hoot: (Not to be confused with a holler) A fun situation that is charged with startling occurrences. Holler is the normal startle-reaction to a hoot.

House Blessing: A technique of clearing-out negative and drawing-in positive energies in order for the occupant to find sanctuary within the home. This is most commonly performed by a Priest, Minister or Shaman on a new residence or after a tragedy.

Human Mind: Unfathomable void: black hole of existence

Hysteria: Extreme panic or fear which may result in the loss of rational thought.

I Ching: The ancient Chinese Oracle used to gain insight into the lessons of man in his quest for Christ Consciousness; based on the Tao philosophy of Yin & Yang.

Infestation: The spreading or overrunning of something to the extreme, so that it is unpleasant and may cause health issues, such as an infestation of bugs.

Inter-dimensional beings: Physical beings that have the ability to move through vortexes from one dimension to another. They are often considered mythical beings such as dragons, unicorns, faeries, and such.

Intuition: Awareness: knowing without reasoning or experiencing.

Karma: The law of cause and effect; action and re-action; the law of contrast. The Universal Law that governs balance, which promotes awareness and learning. Karma is the full spectrum of experiences that lead to mastery of any condition.

Kinnikinnik: The dried inner bark of red alder or red dogwood used in a ritually blended tobacco.

Kirlian photography: This photographic process records energies naturally occurring in living things. When a living object is placed in direct contact with a photographic plate, the result shows an aura-like glow surrounding the object.

Kundalini: The mixture of Earth and Cosmic Energies; Form & Breath; Yin & Yang, total harmony. Chi energy, often referred to as the Sleeping Serpent, flows upwards from the Base Chakra snaking around the other Chakra to the Crown Chakra and returning.

Laser Grid Pen: A high-powered laser which emits a grid of green dots useful for detecting shadows or general visual disturbances during an investigation

Leprechauns: A tribe of small, stocky humans that migrate in and out of Rainbow Vortexes. These are vortexes that cause concave or convex energy flows, which refract sunlight resulting in the arc of prisms that we call a rainbow. Leprechauns are reported to have the technology to create these dimensional doorways but often seem to be collecting precious metals for maintaining this technology.

Ley Lines: Natural latitude and longitude energy lines that create a grid around the Earth. These lines allow the flow of positive and negative energy around the earth that continually circles the planet. Vortexes are created where extreme energy fields are created by like energies intersecting. Such locations are known as power places and in ancient times temples and sacred sites were constructed over them as in the case of Stonehenge and Rapa Nui (Easter Island).

Life Force Energy/Chi Energy: This electromagnetic energy (ectoplasm, as it was once called) is actually animating thought forms and spirits, allowing them to have a small level of substance.

Logical Mind: The level of human consciousness, also known as the Reasoning and Conscious Mind, which processes rational thought. This is the thinking mind which is able to draw a conclusion or resolve problems; the intellect.

Luck: When opportunity teams up with preparedness.

Materialization: The densification of an apparition into solid form using ectoplasm. In this state the spirit can often communicate or move objects.

Manifest: To make real, to create or bring into a physical state.

Manifestation: The process of aligning with Divine Will in order to draw into the physical realm that which is desired.

Medium: A psychic specifically able to communicate with the deceased.

Memory Mind: The part of the mind which records information and experiences, also known as the Subconscious or the Ego Mind. At death, should this part of the mind fracture from the Conscious and Higher Conscious Minds, it will create the phenomenon known as a ghost.

Metaphysics: The study of those things beyond the physical. This open-minded, esoteric philosophy focuses on the understanding and application of Universal Laws.

Multi-Dimensional: Many dimensions (measurements/vibrations) in the one Universe or consciousness.

Nature Spirit: See Earth Spirits

Negative Thought Forms: Thoughts, just as the spoken word, create a tangible vibrational field. These negative or unhealthy thoughts can cause a disruptive energy field and in some case result in a physical reaction such as nervousness, stomach pain and even vomiting.

New Age: The time of heightened awareness when all individuals expand their understanding of self to the spiritual dimension. The Aquarian Age, approximately 2000AD, during which the Collective Conscious of Humanity will reach Christ Consciousness.

Numerology: The study of the vibrational qualities of matter using numbers/letters. It can be used for determining Karma and life goals as well as aid an individual in self-awareness. Numerology is a map to the vibrations that surround us, including our name.

Nymphs: A young female Earth Sprit that appears in either the woodlands or the waters.

Occult: Hidden or secret teachings that must be obtained by using an expanded awareness; spiritual or esoteric philosophy.

Oracle: A wise person or entity with an expanded awareness, often an aspect of Higher Conscience within oneself. An Oracle can be a guide, Master, or angelic being who works to assist the humanity with their spiritual quest.

Orbs: The manifestation of spirit in small, colored, globes that appear like floating lights that can be seen by clairsentients and even photographed; spirit lights.

Ouija Board: A game board covered with letters and numbers used in summoning and communicating with the Spirit World. Most commonly used as a party game.

Out of Body Experience: Experiences attained through an individual's Higher Conscious Self normally when distanced from the physical body. This state occurs each night when the individual has attained deep level of sleep.

Palmistry: The use of the hand to understand the genetic tendencies of an individual. Personality traits and the potential of a person can be determined from the palm using the Law of Correspondence from Hermetic Philosophy.

Paranormal: That which is unknown or uncommon. Para being beside or next to, thus paranormal, next to normal, but not on the mark.

Parallel Lives: Simultaneous lives or individuals that we are aware of and learn from that are not physically with us. This may be an aspect of our own conscious mind that is contained in another living person that we are able to connect with.

Pendulum: A fob or trinket that hangs suspended on a chain so that it can be easily swung in a variety of directions.

Pendulums are commonly used in dowsing or spirit communication

Pet rocks: A nickname given to a helpful stone, especially one to which the user becomes emotionally attached.

Phenomena: Spiritual or paranormal occurrences or activities. Phenomena is just a fancy word for 'what's happening', especially if it's on the unusual or *whack-a-do* side.

Poltergeist: The physical activity that occurs when spirit has access to ample amounts of Chi Energy known as Ectoplasm.

Portal: See also Vortex, Gateway Entrance in which spiritual phenomena is able to pass between dimensions or planes of existence.

Possession: Though extremely rare, this phenomenon happens when a disruptive spirit enters the body of a living person. As the individual must surrender his free will, this mostly happens in cases where the individual is attempting to escape abuse.

Power Centers: Sacred Sites on the Earth where Ley Lines intersect causing an abundance of positive energy that can be utilized for manifesting.

Programming: Energy patterns that condition the individual to specific behavior patterns.

Psychic: Of the Soul. An individual with extrasensory abilities who is able to perceive in a way that is not explainable through known natural laws. Psychic or ESP is the ability to access awareness from an instinctual level.

Psycho-kinesis: The ability to move physical objects solely with the force of will.

Psychosis: A serious mental disorder in which the mind is unable to function and impairs the ability to deal with reality.

Reading: The interpretation of energy patterns on a psychic level.

Reincarnation: The process of coming into the physical plane again and expressing different physical characteristics.

Religious: The act of practicing the belief of another with the intention of attaining the same spiritual connection. The practice of spiritual disciplines of a given faith with the intention of attaining spiritual union with God as defined through another's experience.

REM Pod EMF Detector: A cylindrical shaped box with a small telescopic antenna that creates an electromagnetic field which can be easily influenced by anything that conducts electricity to activate four colored LED lights and a high pitch alert sound.

Rites of Passage: A specific act done in order to allow the subconscious mind to accept that the individual has accomplished all that is necessary to shift into a new level of being.

Runes: An ancient Scandinavian Oracle based on the element of seasons and cycles, used to gain insight into lessons or situations.

Sacred Sites: High energy locations on the Earth conducive to aligning with spiritual energy and manifestation.

Sassoferrato: Giovanni Battista Salvi da Sassoferrato (August 25, 1609 - August 8 1650) who was often referred to by the town of his birth, Sassoferrato. (also known as Giovanni Battista Salvi) was an Italian painter well known for his sweet devotional art often featuring Saints and Madonna. Many of these religious portraits were depicted with halos and the glow of an aura surrounding them.

Sage: A sacred herb used to clear away negative energies and draw-in a natural balance of earth energies.

See: Another term for Clair-voyance or the ability to see beyond the veil into the spiritual realms and perceive spirits such as ghosts and other Apparitions or even shadows of past building and activities.

Scaredy cat: A slang term for a person who consistently overreacts. This term was coined from the way a cat responds when it is startled. Its back is arched, its hair bristles, its eyes becoming large, its mouth is wide-open, accompanied by a shriek and it normally jumps back and shudders.

Séance: A gathering normally at night with the intention of contacting the deceased.

Shekel rubbing: The pleasure of having money available after expenses to be spent on a personal enjoyment.

Simultaneous Time Continuum Theorem: The theory or concept that there is no time, merely a simultaneous action and re-action. A more sophisticated reincarnation theory where-in all things are currently happening, and the individual merely focuses his attention in a particular dimension of reality.

Slimed: A slang term for coming into contact with ecto-plasm. This Chi energy is extremely slippery and feels cold to the touch drawing the warmth out of the body and can give a sensation of dread or disgust

Sirens: A young female Earth Spirit of the Sea. Legend claims that Sea Nymphs are said to have beautiful singing voices that produce a hypnotic effect that often lure sailors to their destruction.

Smudging: Saging or smudging is the practice of burning sacred herbs or incense in order to clear negativity and create a sacred space in balance with the energies of the Earth.

Soul: The eternal personality of an individual, whereas the spirit is the spark of the Divine which gives life to the soul. Thus, the Soul is the core individual and the Spirit is the life force of God that animates the Soul into Life.

Spirit: Any individual which contains the spark of Divine Spirit. Most commonly used to refer to non-physical beings.

Spirit Guides: All individuals, including Angels and Ancestors from the Spiritual Realm who offer guidance and support to each individual within the Physical Realm. They are often referred to as our Spiritual Family or Team. You are the pilot of your physical life, while your guides are the navigator and crew.

Spirit Animals: A Spirit Ambassador that appears in the form of an animal in order to symbolically communicate its skills in assisting the individual within the Spiritual Realm. It is important to realize an Animal Spirit is the spirit of a deceased animal, whereas, the Spirit Animal is a Spiritual Ambassador using animal form to symbolize its strengths.

Spiritual: The state of being in communion with God. The Realm in which all matter is expanded into a collective higher consciousness in alignment with Divine will.

Spook: A slang term for ghost or Spirit, specifically those that have a startling effect.

Subconscious Mind: The part of the mind which records information and experiences, also known as the Memory or the Ego Mind. Of three levels of consciousness within an individual, it is the most immature or undeveloped state of mind. Often referred to as the ego or physically oriented mind—the memory and unreasoning mind—which physically manifests the reality of an individual. Should at death, this part of the mind fracture from the Conscious and Higher Conscious Minds, it creates the phenomena known as a ghost.

Tarot: The Royal Road, a deck of cards which uses symbols to communicate with the Higher Conscious and Subconscious minds. A tool for the expansion of awareness which incorporates the use of Numerology, Astrology, Color, I Ching, etc. to expand or expound on a given situation.

Telekinesis: The ability to move an object using the mind.

Telepathy: The ability to mentally pass messages from one mind to another, often in symbolic or emotional form.

Thingamabob: Gismo, doohickey or the more common term of thingamabob, is whatever physical object you think you need in that instant to get the job done. It is important to note, that as the moment shifts, so does the particular doohickey required.

Third Eye: The Sixth hChakra that is situated on the brow ridge between the eyes. This chakra, known by the ancient Masters as the *Eye of Wisdom*, when open, allows communion on a higher conscious level and the ability to perceive spiritually. It is often portrayed as an eye on the forehead just above the nose or between the eyebrows.

Thought Field: Often referred to as the collective conscious, a thought field is a large area of energy created by strong, focused thoughts.

See *Holographic Universe* by Talbet

Trance: The state of centering oneself and focusing the awareness into a specific dimension other than the rational.

Transcend: To go beyond; to expand one's awareness.

Trigger or Control Objects: familiar objects that adults commonly use or children might be tempted to play with.

Troll: A subterranean tribe of Earth-dwelling Humans. Trolls have the reputation of being grumpy, and prefer living in mines.

Universal Mind: Higher intelligence, also known as the Higher Conscious Mind or Expansive Group Consciousness, is a name given to the mind of God. The Universal Mind is intuitive and gathers awareness directly from the Spiritual Realm.

Veil: A white, gauzy, bridal veil-like drape that sometimes appears with spirit orbs. It can be an indication that the spirit will take on a human-like ethereal form.

Vibration: The expression of Life Force through the movement of energy.

Vortexes: A specific location where energy flows to or from another realm; gateways or portals to other dimensions.

Walk through: The process of walking through a site and noting details in order to make an assessment of the energies within the location.

White Light: Luminescence full-spectrum light which is often perceived as the highest vibration. Since white is the presence of all colors, White Light may contain the perfect balance of all vibrations and therefore be the most pure of the light vibrations.

Yang: The masculine concept, the positive nature of energy. In the Tao Philosophy the aspect of being hot, active, moving, constructive; the spirit or essence of being.

Yin: The female concept, the negative nature of energy. In the Tao Philosophy: the aspect of being cold, passive, enfolding, nurturing; the form or physical aspect of being.

Zapping: To discharge a sudden, focused burst of energy.